TOLKIEN'S
Hidden Pictures

"We need stories to understand ourselves."

—SALMAN RUSHDIE

Tolkien's Hidden Pictures

Anthroposophy and the Enchantment in Middle-earth

Mark McGivern

Lindisfarne Books ◇ 2023

LINDISFARNE BOOKS

An imprint of SteinerBooks / Anthroposophic Press, Inc.
834 Main Street, PO Box 358
Spencertown, New York 12165
www.steinerbooks.org

Book design by William Jens Jensen

Library of Congress Control Number: 2022946837

ISBN: 978-1-58420-895-2

Contents

For Nicholas and Annika,
my treasures

For my good friend Robert McKay,
in gratitude for keeping the long conversation going

Introduction

This book attempts to shed new light on our relationship to J.R.R. Tolkien's *The Lord of the Rings*. Despite the plethora of scholarship and commentary on Tolkien's fiction, I make the case that our felt experience of *The Lord of the Rings* has yet to be coherently understood, and that such coherence is achieved through an exploration of the story's "hidden pictures." The real value of this story for our world has remained elusive, like how dreams can haunt us until we finally map the dream images onto our experience. When we take the feelings and associations of dream images seriously, they can guide us to the right understanding of the dream.

I make two unusual claims. First, the feelings evoked by the story are not primarily a response to its literary merits and narrative structure. Rather, they originate in hidden forms, of which even the author was unaware. Second, of the hidden pictures discovered so far, the one that yields the most value is the one that emerges through the perspective on myth and language developed by Rudolf Steiner, an Austrian philosopher, artist, and scientist who died almost a hundred years ago. Steiner's work was broad, comprehensive, and original. He was a spiritual teacher of the Western esoteric tradition and left a legacy of fruitful initiatives and ideas, including a new understanding of how myth and language reflect the changing consciousness of human beings through history.

The work of revealing and describing inner forms in Tolkien's fiction has been taking place for a while—unwittingly—by a small number of serious Tolkien scholars. I identify this work as a new stream of commentary and I review their findings from this point of view. I then add to this new stream of commentary by revealing and describing a form whose point of origin is a discovery made by one of these scholars.

My goal is not to fabricate an intellectual construct of meaning, but rather to reveal and comment on the hidden pictures within the story, pictures that ultimately bring clarity to the experience of importance and meaning the story engenders. Our strong feeling reactions to *The Lord of the Rings* inform us that something important is present, like the way we experience resonant dream images. Exploring the story's hidden pictures allows us the opportunity to understand the story's importance in concrete terms.

❧

I was thirty-five when I first read *The Lord of the Rings.* I am not sure why it took so long. When I was a child, some friends must have briefed me on its contents, as I have wistful memories of wizards and monstrous creatures momentarily emerging from a landscape of mist and danger, scenes tinged with grandeur and longing. They were dreamy pictures, and I was a dreamy kid. In the end, my Thor comic books must have somehow sufficed, or at least distracted me from a deeper encounter with Tolkien's Nordic-inspired myth. Years later, after reading all of Tolkien's works a few times over, it was clear to me that my own soulful experience of its imaginative power had not been conjured by superficial fantasy. The story had crawled into my soul, gripped the edges, and held on like it had a life of its own. I stood in the world differently knowing that this grand imagery existed. I can still step into it now and feel stirred in the same mysterious way I did as a boy.

My experience is one had by many of the millions of readers of *The Lord of the Rings*. Few stories of the twentieth century have moved as many people as deeply as *The Lord of the Rings*. Its merits as literature have been extensively studied. Tolkien scholarship has achieved remarkable insights into his unique use of language, his deep knowledge of the aesthetics of story within the world's heritage of mythic storytelling, and his ability to weave together the exploration of myriad themes in one story. The turmoil and conflicts of the twentieth century seem to be embodied in Tolkien's depiction of a moral and physical struggle to destroy an instrument of both worldly power and inner psychological decay. It is a tale well suited to the catastrophes that took place over the course of the story's creation, from World War I through to the end of World War II, and to the fragility of the world order since then.

Despite the wide range of popular and literary commentary on Tolkien, the image of his work in the popular mind seems to remain that of an allegorical tale. Yet, early in the history of this commentary, the author himself dismissed the notion that *The Lord of the Rings* was to be understood as an allegory, a form of storytelling he openly found distasteful. He affirmed the notion that his story may be applicable to various contexts, but nothing so specific as to warrant the term allegorical. This left the story open to the charge that, if no allegory existed, it was simply a form of escapism, a fantasy world that allows the reader to apathetically escape the serious issues of the modern world. A series of early commentators criticized the work as having little or no literary merit and its massive popularity the sign of a culture deprived of intellectual standards and thoughtful inquiry.

What rose in reaction to this critique was a new body of work that embraced Tolkien's project as a profound and hopeful attempt to recover a world imbued with meaning and human values. The notion of escape as a serious *response* to the modern world, rather than a retreat from it, forms the heart of the prolific literature on Tolkien's creative genius. While this work has revealed much about Middle-earth, the fictional world that Tolkien created and the place in which he set most of his fantasy works, this same body of commentary has not produced a coherent and comprehensive picture of what this response is. To understand how escapism responds to the world is to begin to understand its meaning and value. Surveying the cottage industry of Tolkienian commentary, one notices the struggle to convey clear and coherent understandings about our experience of meaning and value in the story. I provide examples of this struggle in Part 1.

In Part 2 and onward, I attempt to demonstrate that when the works of a certain group of authors are joined together, a new approach to meaning and value can be identified. When we combine the work of four Tolkien scholars: Patrick Curry, the Jungians Timothy O'Neill and Pia Skogemann, and Verlyn Flieger, a new kind of fellowship emerges—those who share the unique connection of seeing the source of meaning and value in the story's inner pictures.

My contribution to this new stream of thinking is to offer yet another "hidden picture," a new interpretation that considers the authors already mentioned but originates with Flieger's seminal work, *Splintered Light: Logos and Language in Tolkien's World*. My interpretation builds on Flieger's insights regarding the influence of Owen Barfield on Tolkien's work. Flieger claims that Tolkien was essentially attempting to reproduce in story form Barfield's connection between language, myth, and perception. Barfield was a student of the work of Rudolf Steiner. He was also a friend of Tolkien and, along with Tolkien, C.S. Lewis, Charles Williams, and others, a member of the Oxford author group known as the Inklings. After reading Flieger's *Splintered Light*, Barfield himself commented:

> I am more than impressed by this profound and carefully documented study of Tolkien's oeuvre.... It is certain that no future treatment of the subject will deserve serious attention unless it has taken full account of Dr. Flieger's exegesis.[1]

This journey therefore leads us into the unfamiliar territory of Rudolf Steiner's worldview, called anthroposophy, a wide body of deeply esoteric but astonishingly practical work. Steiner's understanding of myth is rarely applied to modern works of fiction though it does contain its own robust understanding of the meaning and value of ancient myth and fairy tale. To bring into focus the core ideas of anthroposophy that we will need, I provide a comparison of Jung's more well-known archetypal psychology and Steiner's ideas about the nature of human beings and myth. My goal is to demonstrate that the anthroposophical view, shared by Owen Barfield, reveals the most significant details regarding the hidden pictorial nature of *The Lord of the Rings*, which in turn can transform the intense but vague feelings of importance, meaning, and value we experience in the story into new insights.

PART 1

THE GREAT ESCAPE

1A. ESCAPISM AS RESPONSE

Tolkien addressed the question of escapism in his lecture *On Fairy-Stories*, presented during a long pause in his writing of *The Lord of the Rings* in 1936. "Escapism" was redefined by Tolkien himself not as the "flight of a deserter," as his critics saw it, but rather the "escape of a prisoner."[2] I take his notion of escape to be, at least partially, the desire not to be imprisoned in an overly rationalized, machine-dominated, and ugly world, deficient—for those very reasons—of any sense for the natural reality and human values that prevailed before it.

Tolkien wrote:

> The notion that motor cars are more "alive" than say centaurs or dragons is curious; that they are more real than say horses is pathetically absurd. How real, how startlingly alive is a factory chimney compared with an elm-tree: poor obsolete thing, insubstantial dream of an escapist![3]

We begin to sense that Tolkien's "escape of the prisoner" centered around release from the subordination of our minds and hearts to the industrial reconfiguration of the world into a machine-driven entity. In this sense Tolkien was a rebel, unwilling to acquiesce to the kind of crass rationality and ugliness that a machine-driven world demands. Lack of imagination is a kind of spiritual poverty that, for Tolkien, effects our practical ability to bring beauty into the world. He also wrote:

> From the wildness of my heart I cannot exclude the question whether railway-engineers, if they had been brought up on more fantasy, might not have done better with all their abundant means than they commonly do.[4]

In this lecture at least, Tolkien shows us that escape is something like a return to a way of perceiving the world that existed before industrialization both swept the physical world and then colonized our way of understanding the value of life itself.

Well-known Tolkien scholar Tom Shippey leads the defense of Tolkien's positive notion of escapism by reminding us that the "dominant literary mode of the twentieth century has been the fantastic."[5] Tolkien's public appeal is not an aberration but part of a larger, "deeply serious response to what have been the major issues of this century."[6] Shippey suggests that one of Tolkien's accomplishments is to have successfully "opened up" the world of authentic fairy tale again for the "contemporary imagination."[7] This line of inquiry takes us beyond the limits of a literary view, for we must acknowledge that the literary form of epic fantasy does not guarantee such an escape, and indeed can often be simple "desertion." Many fantasy writers have imitated Tolkien without producing anything remotely akin to the same effect on readers.

The escape-as-response approach leaves behind discussion of the work's literary merits as a lens on meaning and value. Yet it struggles to establish itself as a coherent approach that can stand on its own. Three characteristics of this weakness appear: the inability to provide a clear alternative to the literary form, a reliance on vague references to the nature of myth to explain Tolkien's appeal, and an inability to describe enchantment in terms of concrete human experience. One example comes in David Day's introductory comments to his excellent book *Tolkien's Ring*, where he shows important and useful links between Tolkien's Ring Quest and the tradition of other ring quests through the ages. Day attempts to

> link the bookish Oxford don who was J.R.R. Tolkien and the wild shaman to a single tradition spanning more than 5,000 years. Tolkien tapping away at his typewriter keys as the wandering soul of his Hobbit hero moves and dances to its pulse is not unlike the shaman tapping his drum.[8]

Tolkien, says Day, "woke something deep in human consciousness through the universal language of mythic images drawn from the early history of mankind."[9] However, *what* he awoke and *how* he awoke them are not given serious attention.

Similarly, in her excellent work on Tolkien's mythological sources, *The Mythology of Middle-Earth,* Ruth Noel traces the use of mythological themes in Tolkien's characters and argues that these motifs and themes explain Tolkien's appeal. Here is a series of quotes that chart Noel's thinking on the matter:

> Tolkien's adaptation of mythology to his works has a profound effect on the reader. This effectiveness is not accidental. Mythic themes deal with the basic challenges that face Man universally and eternally, such as love, fate and death.
>
> Mythological themes are vastly ancient and are a basic part of the subconscious mind.... The study of psychology is doing much to explain the motivation of mythic themes.
>
> The purposes of myth are to glorify history with supernatural events, to explain the unknown and to hallow tradition.[10]

Noel's speculations range from the literary (universal themes) to the psychological (the basic part of the subconscious mind) to the anthropological (the need to explain the unknown). Her definition of myth is only applicable to ancient peoples, not to today's readers. Psychology is given license to shed light on why these themes are evocative but provides little evidence or explanation. The question as to why modern humans would find ancient myth meaningful is not explored.

Randel Helms' *Tolkien's World* is very explicit about the reason the literary form of epic fantasy is not the carrier of meaning in Tolkien's work. He wrote:

> Most contemporary heroic fantasy is vulgar and debasing not because its bare themes are debasing—the struggle against evil, rescue of the good—but because those themes are unsupported by a resonant image of man: they lack a vital superstructure of ideas.[11]

Helms goes on to suggest that such ideas are "large and ennobling" and have a "vision of man's nobility."[12] In short, Tolkien's enchantment works because a view of humans with moral integrity is mirrored back to us, an integrity that we feel inwardly but one that our society no longer expects or wants from us. Helms also writes, "A hero is a culture's expression of our ideals about itself, and our ideals about ourselves have been punctured."[13] These ideals are, in his words, "formulated and understood most efficiently in myth," because myth has the capacity for "discovery, for the transmission of awe, and for molding a worthwhile self."[14]

Like David Day, Helms does not explore a direct connection between Tolkien's work and these capacities of myth. Simply listing the qualities of myth, while helpful, doesn't result in a definition that will in turn allow us to understand mythic content concretely. To know why myth might have these capacities, we need to know what myth is.

1B. A New Approach Emerges

When I studied the group of commentators mentioned in the introduction (O'Neill, Skogemann, Curry, Flieger), it became clear what was missing in the escape-as-response approach. This particular group were able to chart new territory in understanding Tolkien because they had found new ground upon which to rest and support their insights. Where the previous set of authors remained tentative and at times vague about completely leaving the literary perspective, this new group forged ahead. They did not consciously attempt to create a new approach. However, when taken together a new approach emerged. The new ground they discovered emerged because of the following elements. First, they *identify an inner form* within the story that is a possible source of its appeal, given the fact that the literary or "outer" form of epic fantasy alone cannot fully account for it. Second, they *provide a clear definition of mythology relevant to modern readers.* The escape-as-response commentators who point to myth as the way to understand Tolkien's appeal are unable to adequately explain why this may be the case. It is uncommon for literary critics to conceptualize myth in non-literary terms. An added challenge is that our preconceptions about the nature of myth (derived from anthropology and psychology) can in turn shape our understanding of Tolkien's work in ways of which we are not fully aware. Third, they *describe our experience of enchantment in concrete terms.* Given that the sum of our individual experiences makes up the common value of Tolkien's work for our culture, we need clear concrete descriptions of what this experience is if we are to develop a holistic and coherent understanding of the story's meaning and value.

Before we explore this new approach in detail, we will examine the Christian stream of commentary, given that it seems to lie somewhere between the two approaches just outlined, and given the fact that Tolkien himself was a devout Catholic.

1c. Limitations of the Christian Perspective

This stream of commentary thrives because it contains its own understanding of myth and a developed sense of inherent meaning and value as defined by religious faith. In *The Gospel According to Tolkien*, Ralph C. Wood describes his inquiry into meaning in Tolkien's work as a "theological meditation."[15] His project is to "trace the way it discloses—not by overt preachment but by covert suggestion—the principal claims of Christian faith."[16]

In an essay titled "Tolkien, Lewis, and Christian Myth," Stratford Caldecott writes that "each of the four main heroes undergoes a kind of death and rebirth as part of their quest, a descent into the underworld. In this way, each participates to a greater or lesser degree in the archetypal journey of the Christ."[17] Here we see an attempt at identifying an inner structure to the tale that is independent of its literary form. Caldecott succinctly outlines the Christian themes he sees in *The Lord of the Rings*: "choice, free will, and sacrifice."[18]

Myth is the archetypal journey of Christ, a resonant image, arguably for Christians, and perhaps others. However, it does not stand independently on its own merits but relies on a specific system of religious beliefs for its resonance. The fact that the life and passion of Christ parallel already established mythic structures means that the universality of those structures was established before the birth of Christ. With their clear sense of meaning in myth, Christian commentators can marry the Christian notion of the archetypal journey of Christ with various themes, ideals, and virtues from the narrative. The approach is based on themes rather than images.

Other commentators have weighed in on the significance of the Christian view, suggesting that, while Christian elements are there, they are thoroughly mixed with other aspects of morality, ethics, and spirituality. Patrick Curry makes the keen observation that the story blends

> Christian, pagan and humanist ingredients. It is all of these and no single one of them. They can be separated analytically of course but not their joint and mutual effects—any more than can the different flavours that make up a soup.[19]

Meanwhile, Flieger wrote:

> *The Silmarillion* is Tolkien's gloss on Christianity, illustrating its universals, not its specifics. It is concerned, he says, "with the Fall, Mortality, and the Machine," subjects that, in the broadest sense, are the concerns of all myths in all ages.[20]

It seems reasonable to conclude that these authors are correct. The work does not have a predominantly Christian character. Tolkien said he did not wish anything religious to be overt, but rather, "absorbed into the story and the symbolism."[21] The interesting thing about symbolism is that it often has layered meaning, some of which the author may not be aware.

To summarize, the Christian view is limited by its own definition of myth, which does not support a clear description of our experience of enchantment. To say that the Christian values that appear thematically in the story are the source of its enchantment is difficult to sustain given that Christianity is a belief. The archetypal journey undertaken by Christ is an established structure that predates Christianity. The overall body of Christian commentary does not seem to contain content that moves the conversation on meaning and value forward, though it does contribute to illuminating a strong underlying theme. The thematic nature of Christian commentary places it close to the literary stream of commentary.

Part 2

The Discovery of Hidden Pictures

2a. Patrick Curry's Concentric Circles

Patrick Curry's book *Defending Middle-Earth* consists of a rebuttal against Tolkien's literary critics. Curry argues that such critics

> [fail to see that *The Lord of the Rings*] imaginatively re-connects its unprejudiced reader with a world that is still enchanted...a world that is still mysterious, intelligent, inexhaustible, ensouled...a strange world to most of us, but it is also recognizable as one we used to live in but since have lost, although not, it seems, altogether forgotten. And that connection opens the door to the possibility of realizing that our own world (once seen right again) is still enchanted.[22]

Curry's response to this failure is to identify the effects of Tolkien's work in a new way. He argues that there is an inner form within the story that is the source of the feeling of "ensouled." This form takes the shape of three concentric circles: the center circle is the Shire as human community, surrounded by Middle-earth as nature, which in turn is surrounded by the Sea (home of the Undying Lands) as spirit. He argues that it is through the interrelationship of these three specific "places" that we experience a changed perception of our world.

Curry admirably disarms various criticisms of Tolkien's portrayal of Shire life and concludes it is fundamentally an image of human community. Aspects of culture, politics, and society mingle in such a way as to show hobbits as naturally social beings, a reality that strongly shapes their identity and self-worth. He writes: "It includes such things as the hobbits' strong sense of community, their decentralized parish or municipal democracy, their bioregionalism, and their enduring love of and feeling for place."[23]

Middle-earth surrounds the Shire and offers a grander, myth-imbued sense of place. It is nature wrought large in the same way that the Shire is the human world wrought small. The topography of Middle-earth is where our relationship to nature is re-imagined in a new way. The extraordinary detail of Middle-earth is a feature characteristic of Tolkien's style. Curry remarks, "The resulting sense of place gives rise to a startling sensation of primary reality."[24] We feel it as being real. In Curry's words:

> What is most striking about it is the profound presence of the natural world: geography and geology, ecologies, flower and fauna, the seasons, weather, the night-sky, the stars and the moon. The experience of these phenomena as comprising a living and meaningful cosmos saturates the entire story.[25]

At the edges of Middle-earth, the Sea forms the third and last concentric circle. Given its link to the immortal Undying Lands, the Sea has the quality of transcendence—a longing amongst Middle-earth's inhabitants to return to the source of their world. In *The Lord of the Rings*, it is hinted at in beautiful images as the home of the Valar, the spirit beings who watch over Middle-earth. We see that this feeling of an ensouled sense of place is the result of the connection and influence of each of the circles on the other. The living quality of place in Middle-earth is the result of the presence of the spiritual on the outer edge and the human world at the center. If we imagine the qualities of the center and the periphery mixing, we see a world of grounded human reality coexisting with transcendent reality. Middle-earth is a picture of this ensouled coexistence. It is not hard to imagine Tolkien wanting his work to be seen as an enchantment of place. His distaste for the domination of machines is well known, as is his lament at the diminishing natural world and the human values this connection supports.

The limitations of the escape-as-response commentary are absent from Curry's work. Aside from revealing a hidden form within the story, his clear definition of myth supports his picture of enchantment of place. He writes:

> Mythologies, like other kinds of cultural traditions, contain, in coded form, a great deal of feeling and emotion in the form of accumulated human experience: the collective memories, hopes, wishes, fears and dreams of communities across time.[26]

He also quotes Alan Garner on this subject:

> The elements of myth work deeply and are powerful tools. Myth is not entertainment, but rather the crystallization of experience, and far from being escapist literature, fantasy is an intensification of reality.[27]

He likewise describes our experience of enchantment in concrete terms as a change of perception and a consequent recovery of a sense of place, which we can link directly to our own experience. Curry can now provide a reasonable assessment of the story's meaning and value:

> *The Lord of the Rings* is one such vision of an alternative world, where enchantment—communal, natural and spiritual—survives (albeit barely) the onslaught of modernity at its most virulently pathological.[28]

The three concentric circles can be seen as creating an additional experience. The connection between the earthy, communal Shire and the spiritual Undying Lands across the sea is formed through the mythological drama of the middle circle, Middle-earth. Mythology and its enchantment are the necessary intermediary that makes the earthly and spiritually transcendent find meaningful relationship. The earthly experience of an ensouled world is the earthly connection to the spiritual obtained through its experience of myth.

If enchantment can be expressed in the experience of place, what other new perceptions could we be experiencing through *The Lord of the Rings* that would also be consistent with escape-as-response? In the Jungian perspective, our criteria of inner form, defined myth, and concrete description of enchantment are also addressed. It offers a subjective perspective on meaning and value in contrast to Curry's outer, objective sense of place.

2B. A Jungian Architecture of Archetypes

Timothy O'Neill's *The Individuated Hobbit* and, later, Pia Skogemann's *Where the Shadows Lie,* take us on a striking journey through a detailed, coherent picture of Middle-earth as a Jungian map of the human psyche. O'Neill's broad analysis of Tolkien's work includes *The Hobbit* and *The Silmarillion* and dives deep into *The Lord of the Rings*. His approach is based on an initial hunch about the source of meaning. He writes:

> To the extent that there is no allegorical meaning or hidden satire I am in agreement with the author. But meaning comes in various guises and if plot and content are to be taken at face value and simply enjoyed then the reasons for the attraction must be found in form.[29]

Though several authors point to the subconscious mind as being the source of mythic imagination, the clear picture of both personal and collective individuation that emerges from the Jungian interpretation, first appearing in 1978, does not seem to have been accepted as a significant discovery. I suspect this is because it is only within the Jungian framework that the concept of individuation makes sense. It is difficult to see how or why a picture of individuation would manifest in a mythically imbued story unless the whole context of Jungian ideas is consciously applied by the author. This creates a certain conundrum for those wanting greater clarity about questions of meaning and value, for Tolkien did not pursue such a project. The archetypal pattern of individuation fits so tightly over Tolkien's world it is impossible not to see it as a major discovery. In addition, both Skogemann and O'Neill give a clear and reasonable definition of myth, both identify an inner form to the stories, and both can describe our experience of enchantment in concrete terms.

As Jung wrote, "Individuation means becoming a single homogenous being."[30] Individuation is a natural process that occurs at various stages of life but most consciously at middle age. Even then, individuals pursue individuation with various levels of conscious intent. Jung suggested that when individuation is blocked or unattended to, neurosis can result. The cure for neurosis is the individuation process. There is a template to this process. The individual must confront their reliance on a persona, a kind of falsely contrived self, and forge themselves into a self-aware individual. Our sense of self becomes more differentiated through individuation, more accessible to our consciousness. Individuation is the most fundamental of life processes and explains much of the naturally emerging symbolism in dreams, art, and religion. It is central to the human experience and considered by Jung to be of a spiritual nature.

We begin to see the connection between Tolkien's work and individuation when we consider that, from the Jungian view, dream and myth originate from the same place. The generation of both dream and mythic symbolism comes from the unconscious, which is always seeking conscious expression. Myth can act as an experiential template for the reader, enabling them to have a feeling experience of the individuation process as it resonates within the story.

Individuation begins with the emergence of an anima/animus personification, a chance for the ego to see a projection of itself in someone else (often a hero or romantic interest) and begin to feel a connection to a part of itself it doesn't consciously know, rather than continuing its attachment to the shallow persona. Through this connection the "shadow" (one's unknown negative characteristics) slowly emerges. We must struggle with our tendency to project the shadow outward and deny its origin in ourselves. The struggle with the shadow culminates in the encounter with the negative anima/animus, a more difficult opportunity to experience growth. This confrontation is how one brings to consciousness aspects of the shadow, and therefore a fuller realization of the total personality. The goal of individuation is a new balance between conscious ego and the transcendent archetype of the Self. Persona, anima/animus, shadow, and Self are all archetypal realities that can manifest in dreams and therefore be encountered therapeutically and integrated consciously into the personality through dream analysis. Given the archetypal content of Tolkien's work and the specific way his sequence of images mimics the individuation process, the story can be understood as acting in much the same way as a collective therapeutic dream.

Jung reminds us that answering the call to individuation is not a safe decision. It requires courage and insight to successfully shed personas, look at one's shadow, and integrate uncomfortable aspects of oneself. Bilbo's advice to Frodo seems to echo this same call. He says, in *The Lord of the Rings*:

> It's a dangerous business, Frodo, going out your door. You step onto the road, and if you don't keep your feet, there's no knowing where you might be swept off to.[31]

O'Neill summarizes his work in the following way. *The Lord of the Rings* centers on, he notes,

> a few relatively repetitive themes: the transforming archetypes of Self-Realization and the personifying archetypes of the various characters in the psyche. The symbols of the Self—crystal, mandala, quaternion, and the map of the human psyche provided by a complex series of star-sun-moon metaphors, the recurrent union of opposites, and a variety of battling creatures of the unconscious provide one of the most fertile

> sources of archetypes in human expression to be found in modern literature.[32]

Personifying archetypes (archetypes that appear in the story as characters) include the trickster (Tom Bombadil), the wise old man (Gandalf), the shadow (Gollum), the anima (Galadriel), and the negative anima (the spider Shelob). Transforming archetypes, as stated, show up as symbols that appear in processes and forms associated with the full individuation process such as quaternity, the four Rings of Power, various man-made and natural features of the landscape such as river crossings and forests, towers, and crossroads.[33]

The major historical developments in Middle-earth show the fate of the collective unconscious. The shadow of Sauron rises due to the decay of post-Númenórean society. It has become, as Jungians say, "one-sided and unbalanced," for which the consequence is rising conflict with the unconscious in the form of Sauron's slowly growing power. There is a general spiritual decline, signified by separation and isolation as well as an inability to trust and maintain alliances. Elves and men grow estranged as the link to the First Age dwindles. In the words of O'Neill, the decline of Gondor, the flagship of Middle-earth's past, "heralds the emergence of long repressed and denied unconscious complexes, powerfully numinous remnants of the past."[34] The Shire hobbits have shared the same general fate. The outside world is shunned in favour of only what is concretely knowable. O'Neill concludes:

> Their roots were deep in the land but shallow in the psyche, and they were without conscious outlet for deeper motives. The stage is set for a dramatic contest

> with the brooding forces of the unconscious. The goal is self-actualization, achieved through the process of individuation, the re-balancing of conscious and unconscious, ego and Self.[35]

Next, I offer a "story version" of the Jungian view to integrate their insights into Tolkien's fiction. I will draw fully on the work of O'Neill primarily for the personal experience of individuation, and then on Skogemann for the insights derived from seeing the place of Middle-earth as an expression of the collective unconscious.

Jungian Highlights from The Silmarillion

In the First Age humans had a "primitive" consciousness, "awkward and tied to, and dominated by, the unconscious. It is the Age of Elves, the time of the realm of Faërie."[36] Humans have participated in the Fall of Morgoth by the end of this First Age. They are rewarded for their help in subduing Morgoth by being given their own island closer to Valinor, called Númenor at the beginning of the Second Age. Their consciousness expands, and separation from both the elves and the Valar occurs in various degrees. The expansion is so wide that fear of death increases, and thus envy grows for the elves' immortality. The result is disconnection with the archetypes. Númenor is eventually destroyed in punishment for attacking the lands of Valar. O'Neill writes, "But in that expansion the contact with the past and the archetypal substrate is lost; Númenor vanishes beneath the waves of the unconscious."[37]

Those surviving Númenóreans with a remaining connection to the unconscious world set up colonies in Middle-earth and gift them with the symbols and artifacts of the old

Númenórean existence that lay within sight, or consciously connected, to the primeval unconscious. There are two main kingdoms, Arnor in the north and Gondor in the south. A sapling of the White Tree of Númenor, the numinous connection to the unconscious, is planted in Gondor. But Sauron deceives the elves into forging Rings of Power as the selfhood, symbolized by the Rings of Power, of both elves and humans has grown in this land of Middle-earth so distant from the land of Valinor, the unconscious. But Arnor is destroyed by Sauron, which adds to the imbalance of the Middle-earth's collective culture, for of the two kingdoms Arnor was the closer to the heritage of Numenor. The nine kings who take the offered Rings of Power are corrupted by Sauron. Sauron is defeated by an alliance of men and elves, the last time these opposites will be able to unite under a banner of their glorious past. Sauron is deprived of his One Ring of Power and thus defeated. The Ring is lost to consciousness.

The Third Age is a kind of "post-Númenórean" Age characterized by the sad consequences of the Second Age. The Third Age continues the trend of decay as the isolated Gondor is deprived of an heir of Kings, the remaining thread to their more archetypal past. The Gondor heirs of Númenórean Kings follow the same pattern of separation through pursuit of individual gain and material reward, which mirrors the slow return of Sauron, the personification of the ignored psychic energies of the unconscious. As the Third Age comes close to its end, Middle-earth is littered with historical reminders of glorious days of yesteryear, depleted symbols appear everywhere that had once been conscious recognitions of direct links to the unconscious. Their natural numinosity is now darkened and cloaked in negativity. Using the One Ring Sauron seeks to bind these numinous connections in the shadow and making the renewal of the Self unreachable.

Jungian Highlights from The Hobbit

Bilbo Baggins typifies someone avoiding psychic growth. Ensconced within his comforts and having quieted his Tookish yearning for adventures beyond the boundaries of his small world, Bilbo initially refuses the call to growth. Gandalf, as the archetype of the wise old man, opens the path he must tread and gives him a "little nudge outside the door." Once outside the Shire there is only one path forward and that is in the direction of the Lonely Mountain, where the prized Arkenstone of the dwarves rests. The Arkenstone is a symbol of the Self (given the way light and stone are combined, we see the spiritual and material combined) and of the goal of individuation—now Bilbo's destiny. Unconscious energies, long disconnected from awareness and thus now dangerous and terrifying, emerge to challenge this path and train the one who would seek to rebalance the conscious and unconscious with a new self-aware connection.

Once the Arkenstone is in Bilbo's possession, he can, in the words of O'Neill,

> [use the stone to] barter to resolve the political impasse between the Elves and Lake-men on one side, and the Dwarves "under the bewilderment of the treasure," on the other. The Arkenstone is both symbol and instrument of his newfound Self; now he blends the pragmatic hobbit of the Shire with the courage and vision of the Tookish adventurer.[38]

He can return to the Shire richer than he was, his gold a symbol of his new and enlivened relationship to the Self.

Jungian Highlights from The Lord of the Rings

The Lord of the Rings begins in the context of a depleted collective unconscious, a world without wholeness, balance, or peace. In the absence of connection to the symbols of the unconscious, the shadow of the long-forsaken Self emerges in the form of Sauron's One Ring. The time is ripe for individuation. As the One Ring resurfaces, individuation becomes a necessity. The archetypes of individuation must be sought out under the threat of great danger. Frodo, entrusted with the One Ring, has entered the middle years of hobbit life and is ripe for the conscious articulation of his selfhood. Bilbo, his mentor, and guide to the outside world, has readied him with tales about his own adventures. Frodo meets the conjurer and entertainer Gandalf, but soon it is revealed he is much more than that. Frodo learns that this is a disguise for the archetype of the wise old man. Frodo agrees to help from a sense of responsibility, though he remains naïve about the whole picture. In his ignorance of the world beyond the boundaries of his own consciousness, he must trust in Gandalf's guidance.

A transition period is needed to acclimatize the hobbits to life beyond their conscious boundaries. Tom Bombadil is the playful trickster and allows the hobbits a gentle experience of expanded mythic consciousness. They are offered a relatively safe glimpse of the wider cosmic world. Once through this transition the threat manifests in their first concrete danger—pursuit by the Nazgûl.

Aragorn, the archetype of the hero, is the next one to help the hobbits deal with this first threat, though he is unable to protect Frodo from his first wound—a stab by a "Morgul blade." Jung reminds us that pain is the requirement of consciousness, and now Frodo has truly entered the path of individuation. The next helper is of a higher order than human, a truly numinous character, Elrond the High Elf. The road to individuation is laid clear. Elrond clarifies the power the Ring possesses. This shadow of the Self must be destroyed through a dangerous quest back to its place of origin. The dark heart of the shadow must be encountered consciously to undo the path of growing unconsciousness the race of Men has undertaken from the Second Age onward. It is Frodo's task to stay conscious on this path and face all dangers it presents. The path continues with the classic encounters of individuation—positive anima, shadow, and negative anima (Galadriel, Gollum, and Shelob the Spider). Galadriel, as Frodo's anima figure, gives him ego strength by expanding his consciousness even further through images of past, present, and possible future. Gollum, at first just a lurking presence, is encountered and brought into service as he knows the way forward in a manner inaccessible to Frodo. The path of befriending the shadow is central to individuation. Close to his goal, Frodo is fighting to remain conscious and to not be pulled into the power of the Ring. Gollum—the personal shadow—leads him to his critical challenge. The sting of Shelob results in Frodo's loss of consciousness. Once rescued, Frodo is able to continue only with the added strength of Sam's consciousness. Our individuation is not a strictly individual experience. We rely on each other for help.

The Macro View

The Jungian perspective adds insights obtained only by reading the events of Middle-earth from the point of view of the broad history assembled from various texts. For example, the fact that the three elven rings (gifts to the elves from Melkor but hidden before he can bring them under the influence of the One Ring) are being used by Gandalf, Elrond, and Galadriel, and the fact that the One Ring can then be seen as the negative element that completes a quaternion forming an image of the Self. This does not diminish its value to our understanding, but it is a step or two removed from the reader's direct experience of *The Lord of the Rings.*

O'Neill reminds us that the Third Age is somewhat akin to Jung's description of modern human culture. O'Neill writes:

> In *The Spiritual Problem of Modern Man* and other commentaries, Jung discussed this matter of cultural one-sidedness at some length. He deplored the dwindling of conscious symbols for expression of unconscious promptings and despised the chaotic or fragmented nature of modern art when cut loose from the archetypal patterns of wholeness. The problem of one-sidedness is distilled in this idea: simple denial of the unconscious aspects of the psyche does not make them go away—it may indeed cause them to grow more powerful than ever, bringing us increasingly, if unwillingly, under their sway.[39]

The Jungian macro view of Middle-earth in the Third Age is an image of a decaying psyche.

The Collective Unconscious

In *Where the Shadows Lie*, Jungian author Pia Skogemann sees the topographical map of Middle-earth as home to various kinds of symbolism. River crossings mark a "choice of destiny," of which there are four, each at a significant stage in the quest. First, the hobbits cross the Brandywine and leave the Shire behind, a decision few hobbits would consider making. On the border with Rivendell, a stricken Frodo crosses the Bruinen with the Black Riders on his heels. Before entering Lórien, the company must cross the Celebrant. The last is the Anduin, the border with the lands under the control of Sauron. Skogemann says, "The crossing of the rivers is a symbolic expression for a change in the conscious attitude and the result of a decision."[40] Because they are common and accessible to all, they represent aspects of the collective unconscious, as do the towers, broken monuments, and shattered bridges. As the story progresses, these symbols also reveal some of what has occurred in Middle-earth to create the current conditions of the collective psyche.

Next, Skogemann brings our attention to the role of forests. Like rivers, there are four: the Old Forest on the borders of the Shire, the troll forest, the Golden Wood of Lórien, and Fangorn, all of which are, as she writes, "clad in rumours of danger and neither hobbits, nor dwarves, nor men set foot in them gladly."[41] They are "energetic centers in the collective unconscious"[42] with both fearful and helpful powers. In the Old Forest they meet the helpful Tom Bombadil. In the troll forest they meet the elf-warrior Glorfindel. Galadriel lies in the dreamy Golden Wood, or Lothlórien (which Tolkien translates as "Dream-flower"). Finally, in Fangorn, Merry and Pippin encounter Treebeard, the strange but friendly ent.

In the topography of Middle-earth, towers play a significant role. They are usually in some degree of decay. The list includes Amon Sûl, Orthanc, Cirith Ungol, Minas Anor (tower of the sun), and Minas Ithil (tower of the moon). Skogemann sees these as symbols of the

> knowledge and power of the collective unconscious. The decay of the towers reveals how this consciousness has become dull and corrupt over the centuries.[43]

Skogemann then identifies her main thesis:

> [that] the fascination with *The Lord of the Rings* stems from the condition of the collective unconscious in Western culture in our present time, and that Sauron and the Ring express the collective and archetypal shadow, of which we all carry a part.[44]

I take Skogemann to mean that the allure of Tolkien's world is the picture it forms of the current condition of Western culture, to which we are connected and therefore *feel,* just as we can feel our own internal condition. This picture of the collective unconscious is also symptomatological in the sense that what we witness outwardly speaks to an inner condition.

It seems clear that Skogemann's point has merit, especially when she writes the following:

> In the trilogy, we are not confronted with the troubles of a distant past; we are, indeed, presented with the issues of today. What Tolkien's trilogy offers to its readers are suggestions as to how some of these problems might be dealt with, and possibly solved.[45]

Through the Jungian view, myth is defined as an expression of unconscious archetypes manifesting images of the patterns of psychic growth known as individuation. The inner form of the story is an architecture of personifying and transforming archetypal patterns that very closely align with the story's main narrative features. The form is detailed, clear, sequential, and convincing. In their description of enchantment, we are introduced to the important Jungian term: numinosity, which we will explore next.

Numinosity

The hidden picture of individuation has a therapeutic effect. We experience what it would feel like to have our individual potential shift from passive to active. This is Joseph Campbell's point when he says we don't seek meaning as much as the experience of being alive. Our desire for the aliveness of inner growth is stirred when we move through the template of an individuation process.

However, Jung himself valued something more than the therapeutic aspect of individuation. It is important for our study of meaning in *The Lord of the Rings* to mention here Jung's concept of numinosity, for he saw it as the deeper reason we are drawn to individuation. The basic definition of numinosity is a "nod from a divinity," which also suggests its presence. This grew in scope to mean an expression of divine will. Jung used it to describe the transcendent spiritual atmosphere of an experience that is independent of our own will. Tolkien's friend C.S. Lewis wrote about this in *The Problem of Pain*:

> Suppose you were told there was a tiger in the next room: you would know that you were in danger and would probably feel fear. But if you were told "There is a ghost in the next room," and believed it, you would

> feel, indeed, what is often called fear, but of a different kind. It would not be based on the knowledge of danger, for no one is primarily afraid of what a ghost may do to him, but of the mere fact that it is a ghost. It is "uncanny" rather than dangerous, and the special kind of fear it excites may be called Dread. With the Uncanny one has reached the fringes of the Numinous. Now suppose that you were told simply "There is a mighty spirit in the room," and believed it. Your feelings would then be even less like the mere fear of danger: but the disturbance would be profound. You would feel wonder and a certain shrinking—a sense of inadequacy to cope with such a visitant and of prostration before it—an emotion which might be expressed in Shakespeare's words "Under it my genius is rebuked." This feeling may be described as awe, and the object which excites it as the Numinous.[46]

Murray Stein relates the following statements made by Jung to P. W. Martin:

> The main interest of my work is not concerned with the treatment of neuroses but rather with the approach to the numinous. But the fact is that the approach to the numinous is the real therapy and inasmuch as you attain to the numinous experiences you are released from the curse of pathology. Even the very disease takes on a numinous character.[47]

Stein then comments on this:

> If one holds the classical Jungian view that the only genuine cure for neurosis is to grow out of it through pursuing individuation, then treatment based on this model would seem necessarily to include "the approach to the numinous," as Jung states so firmly in this letter. The individuation process, as proposed by

Jung and his followers, typically includes experiences of a numinous nature.[48]

A Few Last Thoughts

To read *The Lord of the Rings* is to have a numinous experience. In the evolution of commentary on meaning and value, the Jungian view stands as a milestone. We saw earlier that when commentators began to explore escape-as-response, they began to leave behind a purely literary lens and attempted to embrace a notion of fairy tale and myth that Tom Shippey describes as "authentic." We see with the Jungian approach a further step taken in this direction. In revealing an inner form to the story that is separate from its literary qualities, the Jungian view separated the impact of image from the impact of narrative. The archetypes exist in a pictorial form. They are understood through their behavior, which Jung spent most of his professional life recording and interpreting. This separation of image and narrative is central to understanding the inner forms and their role in the experience of meaning.

It seems clear that the Jungian perspective on Tolkien has had little overall impact on the general commentary on Tolkien's works, except to support the often vaguely stated notion that archetypes and the subconscious are somehow active in them. I believe this is the case because commentators have not been able to assess the conclusions of these works outside the notion of individuation itself. It is something of a closed system. Unless one is willing to steep oneself thoroughly in archetypal psychology, the Jungian view is difficult to assess or even understand outside of its own internal parameters. The question as to why a strong picture of individuation emerges from the story remains something of a mystery. Why individuation? Is it possible to make sense of this discovery of an archetypal architecture from outside the Jungian framework?

Both O'Neill and Skogemann give reasons for the occurrence of the Jungian inner form.

Skogemann writes:

> Tolkien created a whole fictional universe. The building blocks are, of course, his enormous knowledge of languages, mythology, legends, fairy tales, and ancient poetry. But as he broke down the original buildings and reused the 'blocks' in new ways, and then distilled the material year after year, unavoidable numinous archetypes appeared—just as they did to the alchemists.[49]

And O'Neill writes:

> [Tolkien had,] through years of exposure, an intuitive feel for the elements of myth and fairy tale that influenced the structure of his work without his conscious intent or knowledge.... The structured symbolism would be a coincidental reflection of the underlying strains of commonality, originating from the human psyche and finding expression thus in the story of Middle-earth.[50]

The reader may be unsatisfied with the notion that the inner form "appeared." I find unsatisfying the notion that so detailed an inner form appeared solely from unconscious associations. We might accept such an explanation if no other perspective could be found that might provide more context. Our inquiry may indeed have come to a natural end at this point, with the relationship between the archetypal architecture and Tolkien's *conscious intent* remaining a mystery.

Fortunately, the work of Tolkien scholar Verlyn Flieger offers us a way for the inquiry into meaning and value to both continue and expand in scope and clarity. She demonstrates quite conclusively that, while Tolkien did not have copies of Jungian works by his bedside while writing his mythology, he was in fact studiously applying a different idea about myth and language as a blueprint for his fiction—that of anthroposophist Owen Barfield. The result is the discovery of yet another inner form to Tolkien's work.

2c. Verlyn Flieger's Barfieldian Blueprint

The Ancient Semantic Unity of Language

Flieger's work *Splintered Light: Language and Logos in Tolkien's World* may be the most significant scholarly exploration of Tolkien to date. She studies Owen Barfield's influence on Tolkien's thinking about language and thus his approach to mythmaking. Both men were, after all, members of the Oxford-based literary group known as the Inklings. Barfield saw in Rudolf Steiner's notion of the evolution of consciousness an idea so generative that he spent the rest of his life exploring its implications. He wrote *Poetic Diction* in 1928 and challenged the popular notion that myth was generated by early human beings through the conscious application of metaphors to the natural world like a "coat of paint."[51] Barfield was primarily interested in the evolution of language and thus shared a unique interest with Tolkien—the confluence of myth and language. Using Steiner as a foundation, Barfield postulated that the evolution of language and words reveal how our perception of the world and our connection to it has changed over time. Words once had an "ancient semantic unity," meaning a variety of perceptions held simultaneously by one word, demonstrating that consciousness at that time was substantially different than what it is now. Ancient peoples perceived the world as a unity. Language was born of perception, not abstract application. Language evolved as consciousness evolved. The dynamic behind the evolution of consciousness was the sometimes gradual and sometimes abrupt dimming and fading of the atavistic unity. This evolution meant that the perceived relationship between phenomena also faded to the point that different words were needed to explain changed perceptions.

Flieger discovered that Tolkien embraced this idea. The evidence was twofold. First, Tolkien commented to C. S. Lewis that Barfield's view of language changed his "whole outlook."[52] Flieger reminds us that Tolkien was himself a creator of languages and was pursuing the understanding of language at the professional level of academia. Thus, his "whole outlook" changing constitutes a significant statement. Second, Flieger's seminal work shows how the Barfieldian idea of the co-evolutionary relationship between perception, language, and myth lives within and is played out in Tolkien's *The Silmarillion*. Flieger shows, to a remarkable extent, how Tolkien shaped his own work to reflect Barfield's ancient semantic unity. So, while Tolkien may not have been a student of Jung, he was to a degree a student of Barfield.

Splintered Light

Before exploring the implications of this discovery for the conversation on meaning, let us undertake the formation of a somewhat condensed picture of Flieger's *Splintered Light*. This has some challenges attached. First, the story of *The Silmarillion* is not alive in our culture in the same way as is *The Lord of the Rings*. Second, the application of Barfield's idea stretches over the vast spectrum of time, personalities, events, and hidden meanings. The active principle is never directly revealed, of course. For example, the reader is unaware that the proliferation of names that characterizes *The Silmarillion* is a way in which Tolkien shows how a person or group is perceived by others or perceives themselves. Groups have different names for other groups based on how they perceive them. They perceive them differently based on their point of view and how their own perception changes in relationship to the polarity of light and dark.

Flieger penetrates the surface of events and characters and shows us the active principle that is structuring the story and at the same time offering us a particular experience. Light is Tolkien's stand-in for conscious perception. As light changes so do perceptions, which then influences the formation of words, as words are embodiments of perception. Words form myths that capture in images the changing relationship between perceivers and their world. The dynamic behind the changing light and darkness is the polarity between good and evil. This polarity is used throughout Tolkien's world.

A Summary of The Silmarillion

I will attempt a brief synopsis of the basic narrative of *The Silmarillion* and then follow with a series of quotes from

Flieger that clarify the process of splintering light. After that, I will draw out the Barfieldian structure and theme. But first, the synopsis.

In *The Silmarillion*, Eru, the one God, creates the Valar, his assemblage of gods and goddesses. They sing the world, known as Arda, into existence. But the greatest of the Valar, Melkor, disrupts the singing out of pride. Thus the first polarity of good and evil is formed—Eru and Melkor, with the Valar in the middle. Lamps are placed at the two poles of Arda, but are eventually destroyed by the rebellious Melkor. Light, once embracing the whole of creation, then only illuminates the land of the Valar, known as Valinor, through the creation of two lighted trees sung into existence by Yavanna, the goddess of natural things. This diminishment of light is followed by the diminishment of several voices to one. Trees, meanwhile, are closer to the material earth than the airy lamps. Also, the sap of the trees is used to make the stars, in anticipation of the awakening of the elves in the dark Middle-earth. When the elves awaken they immediately speak in a language, Quenya—a language constructed by Tolkien—that reflects their perception of light. In Quenya, the elves refer to themselves as the "light speakers."

The Valar, however, are not told by Eru how the elves fit into the song of creation. Unaware, they call the elves to Valinor to dwell there with them in the light. But the elves are divided. Some want to go; others stay. As the result, their names change—to Calaquendi, Light Elves, and Moriquendi, Dark Elves. The Light Elves journey to Valinor, and many stay there, happy to dwell in the light. But they begin to show different responses to the call to "see the light," and some, who come to be known as the Noldor, return to Middle-earth.

From the Noldor arises an individual elf, Fëanor, who embodies all that is positive and negative about them. He uses some of the light of the trees to mysteriously craft three jewels, the Silmarils, whose name derives in Quenya from the metal "silima."

The two trees are then dramatically destroyed by Melkor and the monster spider Ungoliant. The Silmarils are the only remaining light from the original source. Melkor eventually steals them and sets in motion the return of the Noldor to Melkor's stronghold in Middle-earth to find them. The Valar ask Fëanor to give them the Silmarils so they can restore the light of the trees, but he refuses. Fëanor's pride and possessiveness of the Silmarils match Melkor's, thus causing a series of decisions that further divide the elves. Flieger writes that Fëanor "embodies the polarity of light and dark." Much evil results from his decision first to refuse to give the Silmarils up to the Valar and then to return to Middle-earth. He also forces all his descendants to swear allegiance to an oath that binds them to recovering the Silmarils. Eventually one is stolen back by the human Beren and the elf Lúthien, and in time all three are put beyond the reach of all beings. One is placed in the air as the star Eärendil, the second is hidden in the earth (perhaps as the Arkenstone), and the third is placed in water.

The elven languages also reflect their divisions. Although Quenya is the language of the High Elves of Valinor, the Dark Elves in Middle-earth develop a language Tolkien calls Sindarin. Flieger comments on this, noting:

> Degree of proximity to the light thus affects the semantic, morphological, and phonological characteristics of each language. The same lessened perception of light that divides Moriquendi from Calaquendi distinguishes Sindarin from Quenya.[53]

Flieger also points out that Sindarin "is formed from [the] Quenya 'sinda,' grey, a word that itself expresses diminished light."[54] To this end, Grey Elves appear in Middle-earth and are called Sindar, and they are the first to speak Sindarin. They differ from the Dark Elves in that one of the Maia (higher spiritual beings, but lesser than the Valar) has journeyed to Middle-earth and joined them. The Sindar never go to Valinor, but instead receive a refracted experience of it through Melian, their queen.

The following excerpts from Flieger's *Splintered Light* add greater context and help to clarify how Tolkien embraced and worked out his Barfieldian blueprint:

> Tolkien's use of light in *The Silmarillion* derives from his Christian beliefs and takes its method from Barfield's theory. His approach is to first restore to words their primal unity of concept and then to set up progressive fragmentation as they express a continuing relationship to the world and a continuing reflection of the light. His technique is conferring literality on what now would be called metaphor and then to illustrate the process by which the literal becomes metaphoric.
>
> The Calaquendi see the light, a perception that is manifest in their speech. The Moriquendi do not see the light and their language is darkened, obscuring their perception. To "see the light," in our world a figure of speech, a metaphor for an inner state, is in Tolkien's world an external reality relating to a historical event,

> while at the same time describing the ethos and cultural expressions of two different peoples.[55]

As noted earlier, the separation of elves into light and dark elves creates a polarity, and these quotations from Flieger further elucidate this:

> For those elves who choose to go to Valinor become separated by the degrees of eagerness with which they seek the light and divide into three groups—the Vanyar (Fair Elves), the Noldor (Deep Elves), and the Teleri (Latecomers). As time passes these divisions become more sharply drawn, until each group becomes an entity unto itself, defined by its differences from the others.
>
> By making light a tangible reality and putting it in the hands of a succession of sub-creators, Tolkien has his reader experience the newly created world of the Silmarillion as Barfield suggests early man experienced his world. What we might be tempted to separate into levels of meaning—literal, metaphoric, symbolic—is presented as a vital whole, a re-creation of the original participation of human bients with their world that Barfield postulates. This is a mythic mode of thought, and in a world where such a mode is no longer dominant, we must call it fantasy. The realistic novel, deriving from and describing a world in which mythic thinking is largely out of fashion, is unable to present such material believably.
>
> Seen in the context of *The Silmarillion*, what happens to Frodo is a logical part of the progression, for his is a story of just such separation and disillusion. Tragic in the context of *The Lord of the Rings,* it is still more tragic as the continuation of *The Silmarillion.*
>
> For the separation which Frodo undergoes from his world and from himself is all too recognizable as the malaise of modern man, in him we experience ourselves.

> And considering the larger mythos, we can understand that this is no discrete phenomenon but part of a continuum that is complete only in that context.[56]

Flieger's Inner Form

By tenaciously exploring Tolkien's "changed outlook" on language, Flieger was able to reveal how Barfield's notion of the ancient semantic unity of language was studiously applied by Tolkien and played a foundational role in guiding and shaping the evolution of his mythic world of Middle-earth. She then discusses how this insight is thematically alive in *The Lord of the Rings*, primarily in Frodo's experience of being separated from his community and then increasingly from himself. She notes, "His journey into darkness takes him away from everything he knows and holds dear, including himself."[57] It is not an inner form to *The Lord of the Rings* as such, but it does shape the main character's journey.

The inner form she discovers is something akin to a blueprint, due to its conscious application. The narrative of *The Silmarillion* is shaped primarily by successive stages of fragmenting light. When the elves appear, their language is immediately determined by their perception of light and their differing reactions to it. A pattern emerges: differing reactions to light shape the formation of languages. The languages too fragment, based on the ongoing reactions to the splintering light. The differing groups of elves then enact narratives that manifest the consequences of their reactions to the light. Eventually the narrative gives birth to stories of individuals who emerge within the groups and shape their own destinies by individual reactions, a further fragmenting from group to individual. The light itself moves from whole to fragment, eventually only existing in its original form within the crystals of the tiny Silmarils.

Flieger's inner form of splintering light rests within and is supported by a definition of myth and enchantment. Flieger offers a few examples of how Tolkien's method relates to our own experiences of enchantment. First, Tolkien has tried to re-create an experience of the "ancient semantic unity" for his readers. He has attempted to bring a feeling for the living quality of language by making language interdependent with myth and perception or consciousness, and not a functional by-product of it. This unity of speech, perception, and story is also used concretely within Tolkien's story by his technique of combining literal, metaphoric, and symbolic meaning. For example, the light itself is literal. It changes form from lamps to trees to sun and moon—and to mineral in the Silmarils. It is also metaphoric in that its splintering is an image of evolving perception. It is symbolic of wisdom and spirit. As a result, we inwardly feel an aliveness in Tolkien's world. Everything is interrelated at every level of its existence. His world is literally saturated with coherent meaning. Anything reductionist or intellectually explanatory is absent. The narrative of *The Silmarillion* is a consequence of living realities within Middle-earth. We learn from this that another aspect of our feeling of enchantment can be the experience of objective meaning in the world.

The terms *fragmentation* and *splintering*, as Flieger uses them, imply tragedy. However, they also point to a creative principle whereby individual consciousness is formed from group consciousness. Group destinies eventually fragment into individual dramas. Although tragedy is plentiful in these tales, the breaking of the original light also, in her words,

> gives rise to the beauty of all the colors and makes possible light of many hues.... Splintering of perception leads to narrowed but also more precise expression, greater variety of words, and an infinite variety of combinations of that mythic grammar which is the instrument of sub-creation.[58]

Flieger points out that the fragmentation and splintering give rise to human creativity, independence, choice, and consciousness. The whole splintering process and all its ramifications is Tolkien's exploration of the meaning and consequences of the Fall—that long separation of mankind from the light of God.[59]

❧

Our Jungian interpreters suggest that Tolkien stirred up archetypes indirectly by applying mythic motifs, narrative lines, and images from ancient myth. They claim his reworking of these into his own narrative generated an inner architecture of archetypes that formed a primary picture of the individuation process. The splitting of light and dark in Frodo has implications for the Jungian perspective. On the level of the individual especially, such a splitting almost replicates the dynamics between conscious and unconscious, which is the main framework of archetypal depth psychology. Though we will later explore the commonalities between the different inner forms various authors have identified, we can already see these commonalities emerging.

In Part 4, I present an interpretation of *The Lord of the Rings* through the lens of Steiner's work. This interpretation is in part a continuation of Flieger's work. She does an admirable job of showing how the process of splintered light carries on from *The Silmarillion* into *The Lord of the Rings*, primarily in Frodo's experience. However, I explore what happens when you take the core anthroposophical ideas latent in Barfield's approach to myth, language, and perception and apply them as their own interpretive framework. We will attempt to draw a link between Tolkien's engagement with Barfield's ideas hidden within *The Silmarillion* and the subsequent hidden pictures that appear in *The Lord of the Rings*. In *The Silmarillion*, Tolkien was consciously applying *concepts* having to do with the nature of language, myth, and perception. In *The Lord of Rings*, however, he was guided by *images*—images, I hope to show, that can be best understood as being formed by and consistent with Tolkien's use of a "Barfieldian blueprint" for *The Silmarillion*.

Part 3

An Indirect Orientation to Rudolf Steiner's Anthroposophy

As a means of introducing the less familiar worldview of Rudolf Steiner, I offer the following as a comparison between Jung's and Steiner's views on various aspects of mythology, including Good and Evil, Soul and the Spirit, the Hero's Journey, Consciousness, and Archetypes. This comparison creates a context through which one can orient to Steiner's spiritual-scientific worldview. Jung's archetypal psychology runs close to the edges of a spiritual view while remaining within the boundaries of scientific materialism. Steiner maintains a scientific attitude and methodology toward the nature of the soul while charting new territory.

In addition, section 3b adds to this orientation by describing how an anthroposophical notion of thinking, feeling, and willing shows up in some examples of modern storytelling. The presence of such images suggests the growing relevance of Steiner's approach to understanding mythic image.

3a. A Comparison of Jung and Steiner on Myth and the Human Being

Good and Evil

Perhaps no simpler definition exists for Tolkien's world than the idea that it is a story of good versus evil. Jung describes evil as being the shadow side of good. The archetype of the shadow is one of Jung's most recognized achievements. He worked extensively to elaborate this idea and describe its individual and cultural manifestations. Evil is magnified when the contents of the shadow are projected outward rather than accepted and dealt with inwardly. Jung was critical of Christianity for conceptualizing evil as simply the absence of good. He concluded that the Christian notion of God as an all-good entity resulted in a compensatory need for an all-bad entity called the devil.

Rudolf Steiner views evil as a polarity in which a virtue is the balance point between two forms of evil; for example, courage is the balance point between recklessness and cowardice. One side of the polarity is called "Luciferic." This is a tendency to inflate the ego and create the illusion of independence from the collective of humanity. It is an illusion that human beings do not need earth existence to evolve. The other side of the polarity is the "Ahrimanic" tendency, a contraction and decay of the ego into its own weaknesses. The Ahrimanic is materialistic and weaves an illusion of humans as simply biological machines with no soul or spirit. Luciferic tendencies inflate the ego into a feeling of individual superiority. The Luciferic separates one from the rest of humanity. The Ahrimanic separates humans from knowledge of their true self, their soul-spiritual nature. For Steiner,

Christ consciousness is the means whereby human beings can find balance between these two tendencies. This balance is the rightful place of the human being. In anthroposophy the Christ being played a central role in human evolution. Through what Steiner refers to as "the mystery of Golgotha," human beings acquired the ability to balance between these tendencies and achieve the goals of spiritual evolution.

The Hero's Journey

Both anthroposophy and archetypal psychology view the hero as the one who journeys into the unknown. For Jung, the hero's journey is an inner trek into unknown psychic territory (the unconscious), characterized by a sequence of interactions with pictorial archetypal representations. The hero eventually returns and establishes a new equilibrium between conscious and unconscious, mediated by the archetype of the Self. The hero is enlivened with new consciousness, knowledge, and wisdom and crosses a threshold into a new phase of personal maturity.

Anthroposophy shares with archetypal psychology the idea that the hero is the bringer of new consciousness. However, the understanding of new consciousness is quite different. Anthroposophy sees human consciousness as evolving over historical time. Ancient peoples once possessed a natural atavistic clairvoyance that was lost in stages. Transitions were marked by the decay of one form of consciousness and a heroic struggle to birth the new. Mythologies capture these historical transitions in dynamic and compelling images, forming a record—as does the history of language—of the evolution of consciousness, the inner life of humanity as a collective. The hero battles with the decaying forces of the old consciousness, using the embodied forces of the new, unlike Jung's hero who only seeks balance with the unconscious. Jung's new consciousness is not a dynamically unfolding progression of growth but a closer relationship with the Self archetype. This relationship does not affect any process in the outer world. The anthroposophical mythic hero actualizes the yearning for new sources of spirit and soul forces. The hero charts the way toward a full transition to a new stage of development. Humanity's stages of evolving consciousness are the same as those of an individual life. Consciousness therefore is a dynamic, spiritual relationship between individual and world. Jung's idea of a "collective unconsciousness" appears also to have this quality of a dynamic self-other or self-world connection. The collective unconscious is defined as a non-personal, genetically inherited, and culturally transmitted reality. Steiner saw the individual as a microcosm of the macrocosmic spiritual world. As such the individual has his or her own spiritual journey that subsists within a larger collective human destiny.

The hero's journey therefore is resonant at the individual and the cultural level. It is an emergent phenomenon felt both inwardly and, in our experience of cultural manifestations, externally. In better recognizing the spiritual macrocosmic impulses of our times we better understand the microcosmic meaning of our individual lives. When we experience strong images of how our individual journeys map onto the unfolding evolution of consciousness, we experience a profound sense of our place in the world and our destiny. In the anthroposophical picture of *The Lord of the Rings* (described in Part 4), we will explore a picture of the transformation of our soul capacities in response to the needs of the currently unfolding era of the "Consciousness Soul." On our horizon, according to Steiner, is the development of a higher form of knowledge called "imaginative cognition." This is our spiritual destiny: to evolve into fully "human" beings by freely developing our latent inner capacities for a higher form of consciousness.

Rudolf Steiner was unique in his assertion that spiritual initiation has been a part of humanity's story from its earliest beginnings and in all manifestations of culture around the globe. The earliest civilizations and societies had mystery centers where priests and priestesses performed rites of initiation. After a preparation period the candidate would undergo a transformation of Self through the experience of a death-like condition. For Steiner, the human being has four distinct though interdependent "bodies"—the physical, the etheric, the astral, and the unique individuality, often referred to as one's "I." During this "sleep," the candidate's "I" (one's unique individuality), astral body (body of consciousness, thought, and feeling), and etheric body (the body of life forces) would be separated from the physical body, as occurs at death. The result is an experience referred to as the "sun at midnight," the experience of non-sensory vision. This experience was transformational for the candidate and when they returned, they were able to exercise new cognitive capacities and "higher" knowledge.

The term initiation lives in our contemporary world as a way of describing events that produce a sudden, often painful, experience of acquiring new transformational knowledge. We often associate the term initiation with traditional cultures who possess rites and ceremonies that mark transitions in the maturation of the individual, often marked by a maturation that includes the acceptance of new responsibilities and roles within the group. The use of the term in anthroposophy refers to a freely chosen inner moral path of exercises that have the eventual effect of developing spiritual organs of perception. The activation of these new organs of perception is initiation. In myth, both ancient and modern, the hero can be seen as one who successfully achieves such an inner transformation and thus brings something new to the world.

Consciousness

Jung saw consciousness as primarily a psychological phenomenon with a static nature, though one that possessed the ability to adapt to changes in human society. Steiner saw human consciousness as a broader reality formed through the combination of physical body, soul, and spirit, and one that dynamically evolved over time. Jung thought both ancient and modern peoples interacted with psychic archetypes in the same way—the Self could project its own content onto the archetype, which in turn generated mythic images. For Jung, mythic images had no concrete experiential meaning in the material world. They were representations of unconscious archetypes only. This perspective is not unlike the anthropological idea, common in contemporary thinking, that ancient prescientific peoples were confused by nature and felt an existential angst over their inability to understand what must have seemed a chaotic world. As a result, they abstracted their experience of the world into a series of metaphors to erect a façade of comforting meaning. They engaged in the same psychic processes modern humans do.

Steiner saw ancient people and their myths in a fundamentally difference way. The self of ancient peoples was different than that of modern humans. There was no individualized "self'" to project in the way we experience "self" today. Individual self-awareness emerged slowly in human consciousness. Again, Barfield helps us understand this. Ancient people "participated" in the world through their awareness of the inner life of the world, a reality Barfield christens "original participation." This is atavistic consciousness—a unity of Self and world in which knowledge is perceived, rather than conceptualized by rational thinking. It was only with the gradual loss of this consciousness that humans birthed rational thinking and the ego-awareness we know of today. One could say the light in the inner world of nature slowly extinguished, resulting in the birth of the light of thought and selfhood. Barfield contends that the record of this process is clearly visible in the historical development of language, which fragmented from an "ancient semantic unity" into a plethora of individual meanings and words. We will see later that this was Tolkien's point of contact with an anthroposophical worldview. Leaning on Steiner, Barfield believed that the contemporary understanding of the consciousness of ancient peoples is woefully inadequate. He even came up with a term to define the mistake, calling it "logomorphism":

Simply put, logomorphism is the fallacious habit "at present extraordinarily widespread, being indeed taken for granted in all the most reputable circles" of "projecting post-logical thoughts back into a pre-logical age"[60] "of surreptitiously substituting our own phenomena for those that [our predecessors] were in fact dealing with" (SA 45). More broadly, logomorphism occurs when we read—anachronistically—into the experience, the thought, the literature of a given stage in the evolution of consciousness, the logos of a later age.

For Steiner, there are three layers of human consciousness. The first is thinking, and we are "awake" to this. The second is feeling, the nature of which we are only dreamily aware. The last is will, the nature of which we are asleep to. This fuller picture of consciousness is also only an image within an even larger one, that of a "higher" self, which we are evolving into through the transformation of our "lower" self. Today, the modern human ego is working on its astral body and slowly transforming it into the first of three higher bodies.

Jungians see consciousness as the uneasy combination of the conscious and the unconscious psyche. It is an essentially static reality whose balance historically fluctuates. Modern consciousness is dangerously out of balance with the unconscious, according to Jung. Yet, this situation is only marginally related to the development of the outer material world. It relates primarily to the subjective experience of human beings.

For Steiner, historical developments are the outcome of developments in consciousness, the symptoms of its workings. He acknowledged the reality of the subconscious mind but did not ascribe the same significance to it that Jung did. Steiner saw consciousness as an historically dynamic reality. Consciousness is evolving in stages. For instance, when Steiner looks back through time, he describes the following changes in evolution of human consciousness: the sentient soul (ancient Egypt), the intellectual soul (Greco-Roman), and the consciousness soul (from 1415 onward). The Sentient Soul Age still has a consciousness of the soul-spiritual world, but it is waning. The Egyptians did not yet require rational thought, as they could perceive knowledge directly. The intellectual soul is birthed by the Greeks, whose experience of rational thought demonstrates a dramatic shift in consciousness from Egyptian times. The Caesars of Rome embraced physical power, conquest, and individual destinies. They held a place for the remembrances of the past, but they had ceased to be strongly influenced by it. Materialism had begun to enter the world and slowly determine the future. In the current Consciousness Soul Age materialism brought the full development of "objective consciousness" in the nineteenth century, a development for the full self-consciousness and individuality of human beings. Materialism, initially allowing for objective knowledge of the world, now becomes so pervasive it works primarily as a corrupting influence. From the twentieth century onward, there is a goal latent in our movement through the Consciousness Soul Era, that of the development of the next stage of the evolution of consciousness, called "imaginative cognition." Of this, Barfield writes (and refers to Steiner):

> In Imaginative Cognition, he taught, one acquires, as it were, a picture-consciousness; it is analogous to the consciousness men have in dreams, and in it the great spiritual facts of life and creation come before the soul in the form of pictures. Formerly the human soul lived instinctively in this kind of consciousness, and the great myths of the past are but lovely crystallizations of its waking dreams. To-day, Imaginative Cognition can be recovered—with the added element of full self-consciousness—partly by definite exercises in concentration

> and partly by letting the imagination dwell on these myths and on the historical events of the spirit underlying them. And it is just these elucidations, from within, of the historical events and processes in the spiritual evolution of man and of the Earth which once found pictorial expression in the myths—it is just these which are scattered in such star-like profusion throughout Dr. Steiner's writings.[61]

In our era of the consciousness soul the mood is often one of isolation and separateness. Barfield continues:

> The human mind feels itself detached from, and set over against, the material world, because it no longer has any inkling of their common origin. We today are less likely to forget the many evil consequences of the onset of materialism than we are to remember that it has also been an essential step in the whole evolution of consciousness. It is not only that without it there would have been no such thing as modern science. Without it there would have been no fully self-conscious, and potentially free, human souls.[62]

Jung and Tolkien can be seen, as my friend Rob McKay said in conversation,

> [as] walking along the borders of imaginative cognition. It seems to me that J.R.R. Tolkien and Carl Jung have a kinship for this reason; they are two of the first individuals in the modern era to find their own way to this frontier. It is fascinating to see that both men approached this destined horizon through forms of play—Jung with his sandcastles and mandalas, Tolkien with his wizards and elves. While Tolkien did not go as far as Jung in bringing to full consciousness the concepts implicit in his imaginative experience, some of

his musings suggest he was aware of the deeper content portrayed in his stories.[63]

Archetypes

For Jung, archetypes are the manifestation of the unconscious, the way we know it is there. Gerhard Wehr, author of *Jung and Steiner*, reminds us that the "discovery of the unconscious" occurred when the new field of psychoanalysis came to two realizations: that the causes of psychic disturbances were not biological, and that the patient was often unaware of his or her own symptoms. At that point the attention of psychology turned to the "soul" or "psyche" itself as the source of the disturbances, and Jung's discovery of archetypes and their patterns emerged as he journeyed past the threshold between conscious and unconscious. Dreams and myth are the primary means by which these two forms of consciousness relate. Image predominates in recognizable, cross-cultural patterns. Yet the exact nature of the archetype remained undefinable. The manifestations of archetype in dream and mythic images were not, in a sense, the thing itself. For anthroposophy, the ultimate origin of archetypes is not neurological, as some Jungians speculate, but rather spiritual. Through his study of synchronicity, Jung himself entertained the idea that archetypes might have a non-psychic reality, a metaphysically disturbing idea for many of his followers.

One can see that the relationship to archetypes is a core difference between Jung's and Steiner's approaches to myth and reflects a quite different understanding of the soul's nature. The anthroposophical view of archetypes is that they are less in the realm of the soul and more in the realm of spirit. Barfield suggests Jung "interiorized" archetypes. Steiner sees the human being as the "archetype of creation," a microcosm of the spiritual macrocosm. The Self that Jung puts at the center of the psyche and the individuation process is, for Steiner, the spiritual archetype of the human being.

Steiner did not see archetypal representations as the core experience portrayed in myth. Myths are representations of our changing perception of and relationship to the spiritual world that results from the evolution of consciousness. Aspects of this relationship have an archetypal quality in that they are fundamental to the human experience. Inspired by Steiner, Barfield described ancient myth as the "ghost of concrete meaning." By "concrete" he meant experienced as reality, not as psychic projection. According to Barfield, the evolution of language holds a perceivable record of the movement from atavistic to historical consciousness in ancient peoples. This record is, according to Barfield, as well preserved in language as ancient fossils are in the layers of the material earth. As consciousness evolved, the principle at play was the gradual loss of this "concrete meaning," i.e., the capacity to perceive the spiritual activity in nature. Myth is the ghostly remains of this once-living perception. This capacity died out, experienced by ancient peoples as a deeply felt tragedy as shown in the tragic death of the gods in the Norse Ragnarök.

Soul and Spirit

Jung's main conception of the soul is that of a psychic map demarcated with a line between conscious and unconscious, known and unknown. Dream and myth are the primary means through which images cross the usually well-guarded boundary line between conscious and unconscious. Freud noted that incursions from the unconscious can appear as "slips," mistakes in speech that indicate an unconscious impulse at work. Jung added a technique called "active imagination," a way of consciously engaging with archetypal images, a method fraught with potential dangers for one's mental health if one does not prepare for the encounter.

Balance between the courageous conscious ego and the numinous complexes of the unconscious is achieved only rarely in individuals, and less so in modern culture, given its preoccupation with technology and wealth. For Jung, the invention and use of atomic weapons heralded a serious threshold in this regard. Our lack of relationship with our numinous unconscious life portends our blind self-destruction. Such is the seriousness with which Jung saw the modern human "in search of a soul."

For Steiner, the soul is the mediator between body and spirit. We experience our soul through its capacities of thinking, feeling, and willing. Steiner preferred the term "subconscious" to "unconscious." Our soul's subconscious component is "below" our waking consciousness, which in turn is below other latent higher forms of consciousness. The soul mediates between body and spirit through three aspects of its nature mentioned earlier: the sentient soul, intellectual soul, and consciousness soul. The sentient soul is closest to the physical body, the intellectual soul is balanced in the middle, and the consciousness soul is more closely related to the spirit. Sentient soul is our ability to feel emotions related to our sensory experiences such as fear, pain, sympathy, and antipathy. Both animals and humans have a sentient soul.

The intellectual soul is our capacity to experience reason and logic. This aspect of the soul allows human beings to experience individuality. We experience "higher" emotions such as compassion through this aspect of the soul. The consciousness soul is closest to the spirit and allows us to be aware of our "self," to be deeply introspective, and to develop imagination, inspiration, and intuition as future cognitive abilities.

❧

In summary, both Jung and Tolkien worked closely with the integrity of image. Jung, in rejecting what he considered to be the overly fixed conceptual framework of Freud, made a notable change to his approach—he played in the sand. In so doing he allowed himself time and space to experience image. His archetypes, as mentioned, are pictorial in nature. He did not try to fit them into preconceived ideas as much as he allowed their behavior to inform him. This culminated in his development of a technique called "active imagination"; a way of engaging with image without overlaying concepts. Jung's conceptual work was based on his reflections, dreams, and experiences, not preconceived theories.

Tolkien, too, discarded the contemporary notion of language as simply a collection of mechanical and functional ways to relay concepts. Instead, he embraced a Barfieldian view that words developed primarily from perceptions—the experienced image. Jung's archetypes, like Tolkien's Faërie, have no definitive definition other than their pictorial representations. Beyond that, neither man ventured. Steiner, however, did venture down that path and spent his life charting the territory he experienced. His modern spiritual path rests on the phenomenological scientific method. Once Jung had enough experience with the phenomena of synchronicity, he began to speculate that the archetypes must have an objective existence outside the individual psyche, a step that brought him closer to Steiner's notion of a human spiritual archetype. Tolkien's Christian faith offered him a wider religious outlook on human imagination, which he saw as a "sub-creative" force in relation to the creative force of God. His outlook also kept him open to how the spirals of our development would bring us back to God different from when we left, as close an endorsement of the notion of evolving consciousness as a Christian might attain.

Jung constructed a phenomenologically based approach to working with the unconscious by taking seriously the behavior of archetypal imagery in dreams, art, and religion. Tolkien painstakingly incarnated his image-laden vision of Middle-earth using the principle of the unity of language, myth, and perception.

3B. Images of the Threefold Soul in Modern Storytelling

The foundation of my anthroposophical interpretation of *The Lord of the Rings* is the representation of the three main characters as images of the soul capacities of thinking, feeling, and willing. At first this may sound farfetched, perhaps a reading of anthroposophy into the text. To address this let me begin by demonstrating in a series of examples how this same characterization is showing up in other stories of our time. My personal belief is that this is a relatively new phenomenon, and that it relates to Tom Shippey's insight that the re-emergence of the "fantastic" is the dominant mode of literature in the twentieth century. I suspect this shift to fantasy is a re-emergence of mythic image as a means to comprehend the accelerated change occurring since the dawn of the twentieth century, which is in turn a symptom of a new kind of consciousness struggling to manifest in human culture. All the stories I will mention below have changing consciousness as a main theme.

First, let us explore one of the main storytelling experiences of my youth in the 1960s, the well-known television series *Star Trek*. When one contrasts the characters of Spock, Dr. McCoy, and Scottie we see a clear delineation of thinking, feeling, and willing. Spock is intellect, McCoy is heart and emotion, Scottie, as engineer, is the will, in the sense that he has been charged with care over the movement of the ship. Captain Kirk, of course, is the ego-consciousness that takes input from these three main characters and makes thoughtful and insightful decisions based on their help. He balances the strong tendencies of each and then resolves situations through his own inner judgment. The crew members often re-evaluate themselves and their own human tendencies and characteristics when faced with examples of both higher and lower forms of consciousness.

A more recent example is the popular children's Christmas story *The Polar Express*. In it, a young boy is teetering on the edge of not believing in Santa Claus. In the film version, the boy meets three other children on the train to the North Pole: a nerdy factfinder, an empathetic girl, and a weak boy who struggles to find the inner and outer will to board the train. The main character's meeting with Santa Claus allows him a gentle transition to the next stage of life, all the while preserving his reverence for the mystery of life.

Another example is the American classic *The Wizard of Oz*. In this film we see three characters encountered by the farm girl Dorothy: the Scarecrow who needs a brain (thinking), the Tin Man who needs a heart (feeling), the Cowardly Lion who needs courage to act (willing). Interestingly, Dorothy's house lands on the Wicked Witch of the East, killing her. The tension between East (older, atavistic consciousness) and West (modern consciousness) is already evident. Dorothy undertakes a quest to find the needed brain, heart, and courage. She must help each of the other three overcome their weakness. In the end she can show them that these are inner capacities rather than outward realities. The encounter with the Wizard is an encounter with her higher self, yet nearer the beginning of the story, the Wizard was seen as a kind of almost unreachable, mysterious entity. But by the end, after several trials, the Wizard has lost his otherworldly mystery and becomes accessible. The powers of the Wizard end up being the simple ability to confide to each character the qualities they have already earned for themselves. Thus, Dorothy, with her ego newly matured, can now confront the Wicked Witch of the West, the shadow of her strengthened ego. She returns "home" to her everyday consciousness. Her incantation, "There's no place like home," can be understood as follows: "I am now in the right relationship to myself for the life I am to lead."

As a final example, the 1999 film *The Matrix* has been beautifully revealed by Seth Miller to contain a framework of anthroposophical pictures of the human being. *The Matrix* trilogy is a complex narrative. In summary, one could say it is a story of how artificial intelligence takes over the human race. The sky has been darkened and the only energy source for the machines is human beings. Humans are "grown" for their electrical energy and controlled through a system of mind control, called the Matrix, to believe they are living normal lives. Yet humans have found a way to rebel against the machines. Two rebels, Morpheus and Trinity, release Neo from the Matrix, thinking he is "the One"—chosen to overcome the machine world.

Miller's treatment of *The Matrix* trilogy is sophisticated and best read in its essay form (see bibliography). A summary would include how the main character, Mr. Thomas A. Anderson—Neo's born name—is asleep to his inner nature as the One and is woken from his deadening life in the Matrix, through a series of transformations, to his destiny. Along with Trinity and Morpheus, he is part of a trinity of characters who make up the core dramatic content of the story. Miller shows in detail how each character is an image of one of our three soul capacities: Morpheus is thinking, Trinity is feeling, and Neo is willing. In the first film, Thomas Anderson is transformed from being an "everyday common person," smothered by conformity, into "the One," a true individual who begins to create his own destiny. His training with Morpheus is a training in "freeing his mind" from what he thinks to what he knows:

> After taking the red pill (the pill of Lucifer, of knowledge of the spiritual world), Neo undergoes a process of intense training. His eyes are closed, and like a meditant he is involved in transforming his thinking. Although he knows intellectually, abstractly, that the Matrix is not what it seems, he must sublimate this understanding through a real transformation of his thinking life. This occurs particularly clearly in the martial arts training program with Morpheus, where Neo is admonished into realizing that it is not what he thinks but what he knows.[64]

He is shot and "dies" in the Matrix but is resuscitated by Trinity and is able then to see the computer code that lies behind the images of "reality" being generated by the Matrix. This is an image of his transformed thinking from intellect to an ability to see the spiritual archetypes behind the image of existence—imaginative cognition.

The whole story is a picture of the transformations of each capacity: thinking (through the saving of Morpheus), then feeling (through the resuscitation of Trinity's heart), and then the will through "the One's sacrifice of his body" to become something new. This is but a glimpse into a complex story. However, the way in which Miller's revealing of the story's hidden pictures aligns with all the salient details of the story tells us his efforts are worth careful consideration.

As mentioned, each story discussed here shares the theme of changing consciousness. Initiatory dangers are faced and transitions to new identities are enacted. Knowledge of the soul world is gained. *The Polar Express* presents the simplest image—a young boy on the cusp of not believing in Santa Claus, his life of early imagination shifting into the next stage of growing up. *Star Trek* is a series of stories of modern ego-consciousness encountering other forms of consciousness in the galaxy and being influenced and affected by this exploration. To "boldly go where no one has gone before" could easily be read as a statement of a quest for a new consciousness. *The Wizard of Oz* shows us a young girl transitioning from adolescent to the ego-consciousness of adulthood. It is a picture of finding our true home—our real identity—within a right relationship to our thinking, feeling, and willing. And Neo of *The Matrix* trilogy transcends the hold that the machine world has on human beings. In the process he dispels the reigning system that sees human beings as being like biological machines and lacking free will. His will is awakened through an initiation into the difference between image and reality, and he is then able to transform himself into a new ("Neo") being, that is, one with new capacities of imagination, inspiration, and intuition.[65]

The presence of images of a threefold human soul and their connection to the theme of changing consciousness suggests that the modern literary engagement with the "fantastic," as Shippey said, might in fact be an active intuition that seeks new knowledge of the human being through the exercise of imagination.

Part 4

The Hidden Picture of Spiritual Initiation Revealed through Rudolf Steiner's Anthroposophy

We will now turn our attention to a new inner form within *The Lord of the Rings.* Broadly speaking, it consists of three processes we can identify as coming uniquely from anthroposophy. The first is the formation of an image of the modern human soul based on how the three main characters portray thought, feeling, and will. The second is an image of the evolution of consciousness, also portrayed through three characters, which provides the proper context for the One Ring to be both understood and defeated. The third is an image of three initiations undertaken by the three main characters that lead to the birth of a new era.

4a. *The Fellowship of the Ring* as an Image of Our Soul Nature

Frodo is often seen as the central character of *The Lord of the Rings.* While much of the story is seen through his eyes, the story isn't only structured around his experience. The Fellowship of the Ring is a group, and the efforts of the group, as a whole, center around a common purpose in which all share an equal commitment and conviction.

Looking closely at the Fellowship, there are three central characters around whom the others are gathered. Gandalf, Aragorn, and Frodo make up the pillars of the fellowship, and it is their unity of purpose that forms the group's nucleus. Frodo has his three hobbit friends, and Aragorn has his elf and dwarf. Only Gandalf can stand unsupported. Since Frodo's attitudes and experience most resemble our own, he forms our entry point into the story. Each character brings separate though complementary capacities. Gandalf provides knowledge, judgment, and insight. Aragorn brings strength, loyalty, and courage. Although Frodo "knows not the way," he freely assumes the role of Ring-bearer, knowing he is likely being asked to walk beyond the clearly marked boundaries of the hobbit character. Each character has their own distinctive developmental tasks, challenges, and destinies. However, they realize that in this fateful hour they belong together in fellowship. In this bonding, an image of the human soul emerges: Gandalf is an image of the soul capacity of thinking; Aragorn is the soul capacity of feeling; and Frodo is the soul capacity of willing. They each exemplify a strong tendency toward one of these three capacities. Gandalf is the leader, Aragorn the protector, and Frodo the bearer. As leader, Gandalf is entrusted with the role of providing guidance, judgment, and strategy—all thinking qualities. Aragorn is entrusted with defending the Fellowship from its enemies. He will be required to bring forth immense courage in battle and steadfast loyalty to both the goals of the quest and his hidden royal identity. Frodo is entrusted with physically getting the Ring to a specific location. It is only Gandalf, Aragorn, and Frodo who will later encounter and pass through death-like experiences, the hallmark of initiation. Each initiation experience will occur in such a way as to again reveal the role of each character as one aspect of a threefold image of the human soul nature. Each initiation experience is a dramatic highpoint in the story.

Gandalf: An Image of Thinking

Gandalf's task in Middle-earth is to provide guidance, which he can only accomplish by constantly traveling, by deeply reflecting on events, and through interpreting the motivations and actions of the different characters. His title, the Grey Pilgrim, reveals this. The color grey signifies a lack of absolute knowledge, whereas the word "pilgrim" signifies travel. Gandalf is constantly weaving together objective information with his own insights to keep one step ahead of the workings of Sauron. Through his constant travel he demonstrates an open-mindedness to all sources of knowledge and wisdom in Middle-earth. He displays a strong tendency to allow the world and its events to speak to him and influence how he thinks and what he thinks about.

Whereas Gandalf has deep insight and knowledge regarding the destiny of Middle-earth, his guidance remains based on his own abilities as a wizard to work with knowledge and to think through the implications of different courses of action. Thus he is vulnerable to error and to losing his connection with the source of wisdom that is part of his original nature. As one of the Istari (angelic beings), Gandalf is aware of the big picture in Middle-earth. He displays a kind of instinctual feel for how all the seemingly diverse elements fit together. But as a wizard sent into a particular historical situation, he must use his thinking capacity to be his own guide. We never see him implore or seek out a higher power, except another wizard, to assist him in his decision making. Although he is aware that higher forces are active and can be seen in the workings of "chance," he doesn't depend on them to accomplish his goals. There is a richness to Gandalf's thinking that engenders trust. He tells Frodo that he has decided to join the Fellowship because "someone said that intelligence would be needed."[66] By the end of the story, he has orchestrated the defeat of Sauron mainly through the relationships he has nurtured with other beings and through his ability to unite them with a clear conception of the purpose of the quest, rather than through the higher powers he possesses.

Aragorn: An Image of Feeling

Aragorn first appears as a shadowy, mysterious friend of Gandalf. He slowly reveals more of his identity to the hobbits on the way from Bree to Rivendell. Frodo and Sam learn that Strider, the name by which they first know him, is a Ranger of the North with a detailed knowledge of Middle-earth folklore. Strider's real identity is only hinted at in Gandalf's letter to Frodo in Bree. He writes, "All that is gold does not glitter, not all those who wander are lost."[67] There is something hidden about Strider, something secret.

From the beginning Strider displays an intensity of feeling just below the surface. The hobbits see this on the way to Rivendell:

> As Strider was speaking they watched his strange eager face, dimly lit in the red glow of the wood-fire....The hobbits looked at him, and saw with surprise that his

> face was drawn as if with pain, and his hands clenched the arms of his chair.[68]

His real identity is hidden, and we sense from Gandalf's letter that there is a high purpose in this identity and in his destiny. The letter is worded so that it conveys a strong feeling about Aragorn without revealing any concrete information.

As the story progresses, he sees that the qualities of a king reside in Aragorn's feeling life. There is nothing in his outward appearance or station in life that even hints at his real identity. We see these regal qualities externalized only rarely and in glimpses suddenly reflected in his face and posture. Aragorn lives a life of emotional commitment to his inner identity.

Like Gandalf he is constantly moving through Middle-earth. At one point in the story, we see Aragorn's movement in a particular light that displays his image of heart feeling. Aragorn, Legolas, and Gimli chase the Uruk-hai, who have captured Merry and Pippin; they run for three days and nights without stopping. While elves and dwarves may naturally possess such abilities, for a human man to do this feels more symbolic. The heart is the one part of our body that works continually without rest.

Frodo: An Image of Will

Unlike Gandalf and Aragorn, Frodo's identity is intimately linked to his home, the Shire. The wandering Gandalf and Aragorn stand in stark contrast to the homebound Frodo, who, like Bilbo before him, is reluctant to leave the confines of his comfortable and peaceful life. Frodo is deeply attached to his small network of rural villages developed within the rhythmic pace of a natural, agricultural setting.

The rhythmic pace of agricultural life defines the hobbit character. While the Shire is sleepy and predictable (so much so that Frodo thinks an invasion of dragons would be a good idea) it has nourished a quality of will in the hobbits that only Gandalf has the intuitiveness to recognize.

Life follows rhythm and patterns. While our thoughts and emotions "wander," our will capacity is strongly related to the formation of habits that are formed by rhythmical repetition. Like the hobbits, we often define ourselves by the habits that our culture and experience of life provide for us. Habitual behavior is difficult to transform. The hobbits are reluctant to leave the rhythms of life that give them a stable and secure sense of self.

Yet, it is precisely this quality of will that Gandalf deems important in the hobbits and upon which he will base the hopes of the Ring Quest. Gandalf has perceived that something unexpected lies under the habitual skin of the hobbits. He senses a hidden capacity for resolve, endurance, and resourcefulness that can be activated in times of need—all qualities of our will-nature. Gandalf says to Frodo:

> Hobbits really are amazing creatures.... You can learn all that there is to know about their ways in a month, and yet after a hundred years they can still surprise you at a pinch.[69]

But deep these qualities lie, and Gandalf will face many objections to trusting the hobbits with serious responsibilities.

Gandalf knows that Frodo must make the decision to be involved with the Ring out of his own free will. If Frodo is forced or manipulated to go, Gandalf knows that he would long too much for the familiar, for that sense of self that is attached to the Shire.

Frodo's encounter with the Black Riders between the Shire and Rivendell gives us a forewarning of the challenge the quest holds for him, and his actions during the encounter underlie the image of will that he reflects in the story. The sting of the Black Rider's knife leaves Frodo in a death-like chill. The wound temporary paralyses his arm and shoulder, and with a weakened will the journey for Frodo to Rivendell is much harder. Aragorn sees the same quality emerge that Gandalf has seen. Aragorn comments:

> Frodo is made of sterner stuff than I had guessed, though Gandalf hinted that it might prove so. He is not slain, and I think he will resist the evil power of the wound longer than his enemies expect.[70]

The encounter with the Black Riders shows Frodo's challenge to be a physical one. It resides in his capacity to physically make the journey to Mordor. Although his body is the object of attack, Frodo's sterner stuff, his will, rises to meet the challenge and defines his role in the Fellowship.

Steiner suggested that thought, feeling, and will as a group relate to our modern consciousness in the following way. In thought we are most awake. In feeling we dream. In our will we are asleep. This breakdown seems to correspond well to our three main characters. Gandalf is indeed the most awake of the group, its natural leader. Aragorn pursues the dreamy idea that he may transform from a lowly ranger into the King of the land. Frodo falls in and out of sleep several times and is the one least aware of the full nature of the quest. He only gradually grasps the full extent of what is at stake, mostly through Galadriel's help. He is the one who must go through the most darkness with the least light. The term "ringbearer" emphasizes will. His role is not to figure out what to do, just to do it. He trusts the leadership of Gandalf and the courage and fortitude of Aragorn.

I wonder if the equal incorporation of will into this picture is a result of Tolkien's serious Catholicism. God's will is the guiding light for Catholics, and our own will is called upon continuously in the Gospels. I think it likely that Tolkien saw the quality of will as a central attribute of human beings.

In summary, the Fellowship of the Ring is an image of the soul. This image consists of three distinct but interrelated capacities, each represented by a specific character. In the fellowship we feel the unity of our own soul nature.

4B. The Road to Rivendell: From Atavistic to Historical to Transformational Consciousness

As Gandalf, Aragorn, and Frodo come together to form an image of the human soul, they encounter three unique individuals before the quest truly begins: Tom Bombadil, Elrond, and Galadriel. The four hobbits encounter Tom as they leave the Shire and before they reach Bree. At the Council, Tom is also discussed, as are Saruman the White and Gollum. The movement from Tom to Elrond to Galadriel is a movement through three forms of consciousness: from atavistic to historical to transformational. At Rivendell, reflection on the actions of Saruman and Gollum is central to determining the decision to destroy the One Ring. Saruman and Gollum show us different manifestations of evil, which leads the Council toward the realization that a Fellowship of the Ring is necessary. The encounter with Galadriel at Lothlórien brings the quest into its fullest expression. Gifts are given that prove essential to its success, while the roles of Tom and Elrond fade completely from the story.

Tom Bombadil's Atavistic Consciousness

On the way to Rivendell, Frodo and the hobbits encounter a unique individual. Tom Bombadil is not often given much consideration in Tolkienian commentary and was even left out of the film adaptations. The first thing we notice about Tom Bombadil is that song, rhythm, and dance are his natural way of being in the world. When he rescues Merry from the clutches of the Old Man Willow using the power of speech alone, the hobbits realize that Tom is no ordinary woodsman. Dancing, singing, and reciting poetry, Tom leads the hobbits to his home. He seems to have more than just a deep knowledge of the Old Forest. He relates to the world through rhythm. In his very way of being there is a connection with his environment that goes beyond knowledge. It isn't long before the hobbits are prompted by curiosity to ask him exactly who and what he is. In Tom's response we begin to get a sense of how he perceives the world. He says, "Eh, what? Don't you know my name yet? That's the only answer."[71] To the same question Goldberry only replies, "He is." Then she adds, "He is, as you have seen him....He is Master of wood, water, and hill."[72] We learn from this an important fact: that Tom and Goldberry are not self-conscious of their identities.

Tom tells the hobbits that he existed first in Middle-earth:

> Eldest, that's what I am. Mark my words, my friends: Tom was here before the river and the trees; Tom remembers the first raindrop and the first acorn.[73]

Initially very little about Tom or their encounter with him seems to make sense. However, if we see the link between Tom's perception of the world and his perception of himself, then we begin to understand him and his significance to the story. Tom's rhythmical state of being reflects the rhythmical element of the natural world. He does not perceive a difference between himself and nature. He relates to it as if he and the world were a unity. His age tells us that his way of understanding is an ancient one. The obvious conclusion is that Tom's way of perceiving the world has not changed since the beginning of history. Tom lives in a state of consciousness from when Self and the world were unified. He is defined by his unity with the world, not by a sense of personal identity. Tom would fit a characterization of Owen Barfield's idea of original participation, namely that human beings began their historical existence, as a child does, without an awareness of individual Self. We sense that Tom's lack of ego-consciousness, expressed in his answer to who he is, is related to his symbiotic relationship to the Old Forest. It is as though Tom's identity is not individualized but diffused within his environment.

Consider the following passage where the hobbits are listening to Tom speak:

> When they caught his words again they found that they had now wandered into strange lands beyond their memory and beyond their waking thought, into times when the world was wider, and the seas flowed straight to the western Shore; and still on and back Tom went singing into ancient starlight, when only the Elf-sires were awake. Then suddenly he stopped, and they saw that he nodded as if he was falling asleep. The hobbits sat still before him, enchanted; and it seemed as if,

> under the spell of his words, the wind had gone, and the clouds had dried up, and the day had been withdrawn, and darkness had come from East and West, and all the sky was filled with the light of white stars.[74]

Using Barfield's idea of original participation, we could understand this passage in the following way: that going beyond "waking thought" would be a reference to a state of consciousness preceding a logical, rational, "wakeful" way of thinking. Also, the phrase "when the world was wider" could be a reference not to the physical world but rather our perception of it. A wider perception could mean a perception that included more than just physical matter. And the phrase "[when] seas flowed straight to the western Shore" could be understood as a time when human consciousness was connected directly to the spiritual world. Interestingly, the end of this passage is written in such a way as to suggest that the natural world is responding to Tom's words, as if to emphasize their union.

Tom's dreamy description of the Elder Days enchants the hobbits and they would no doubt have liked to consider Bombadil an ally in their quest. Surprisingly, Tom is indifferent to the Ring Quest. Tom holds up the Ring and jokingly makes it disappear in a bit of mocking hand magic. Frodo is annoyed at this and the hobbits in general are somewhat alarmed. Interestingly, Tom is the only one who can see Frodo when he has the Ring on, and is the only one who doesn't disappear when wearing it. Tom is outside the influence of the Ring. The hobbits realize that Tom can be of no help with the Quest, not because of any intended malice on his part, but simply because he is unable to comprehend its significance. Tom is both unwilling and unable to rouse his consciousness out of the nature-rhythms of its existence. This fact is underlined by Gandalf during the Council of Elrond. Gandalf clarifies for the Council the true nature of Tom's consciousness and why he will be ineffectual in the Ring drama. Gandalf says that if Tom had been invited to the Council,

> He would not have come.... The Ring has no power over him. He is his own master. But he cannot alter the Ring itself, nor break its power over others.[75]

And in answer to whether Tom could keep the Ring hidden and safe, Gandalf replies:

> No. Not willingly. He might do so...but he would not understand the need. And if he were given the Ring, he would soon forget it, or most likely throw it away. Such things have no hold on his mind.[76]

Our knowledge of Tom Bombadil is that of an old, enchanting, but deeply atavistic consciousness, out of step with the current dynamics of evil. Dignified, benevolent, and in some ways wise about the world, Tom is nevertheless lacking a crucial capacity—the ability to see himself as separate from the world. In this separation, consciousness of self develops, as does an understanding of how evil works in the current time.

After crossing the "threshold" of "golden light" (an image of original participation) in the house of Tom Bombadil, the hobbits journey on to Bree, with its "doors looking westward" (modern self-consciousness).[77] Here the drama really begins, as Bree is on the edge of the Shire, the edge of what has until now been the known world of the hobbits. Tolkien's most definitive statement concerning Tom

Bombadil was that he is a "reflection of the spirit of the vanishing Yorkshire country-side."[78] But what is the spirit of the countryside? It could be understood as beauty that was surely vanishing in Tolkien's day. We could also take the meaning of "spirit" to be the way of being that rural, premodern life nurtured. In this sense Tom could be seen as a reflection of that spirit. For the hobbits and for us, Tom's being reflects a different consciousness, one shaped by forces quite different from those that determine the historical conditions of the present day.

Elrond's Historical Consciousness

After the encounter with Tom, the main characters meet in Rivendell, the house of Elrond the High Elf. Elrond is presented to us as a kind of historical sage. He has lived, like Bombadil, since the First Age of Middle-earth. But unlike Bombadil, Elrond has played an active role in historical developments. As an immortal elf, he has been physically present at decisive moments, most notably when Isildur cuts the One Ring from Sauron's hand but does not destroy it.

Elrond's active involvement in each historical age has allowed him to accumulate knowledge and insight into the dynamic events that have shaped Middle-earth. His way of thinking and being is intimately connected to how the world changes over time. Most of Elrond's words and actions come from this living awareness. He says:

> But my memory reaches back even to the Elder Days. Eärendil was my sire, who was born in Gondolin before its fall; and my mother was Elwing, daughter of Dior, son of Lúthien of Doriath. I have seen three ages in the West of the world, and many defeats, and many fruitless victories.[79]

The Council opens with Elrond's account of the beginning of the Second Age, when Sauron created the Rings of Power. Conflict over the Rings dominates the history of this Age, but we can also see an important development occurring: the theme of separation. In the Second Age we see the focal point of action take a geographical shift away from Númenor, an island kingdom that once had a distant but still direct relationship to the Undying Lands of the Valar: "Of Númenor he spoke, its glory and its fall, and the return of the Kings of Men to Middle-earth out of the deeps of the Sea, borne upon the wings of storm."[80]

The Third Age is a time when the ancient and direct connection with Valinor is slowly dissolved and almost forgotten. While the Second Age saw what was known as a "Last Alliance between Elves and Men," the Third Age sees even this connection with the elves cut. Men are standing increasingly alone in the world. The world of the spiritual beings, the Blessed Realm, is now only remembered in legend and myth.

Taken as a whole, we can see that a separation occurs between Valinor and the rest of the world, geographically in the Second Age, then spiritually in the Third Age. The focal point of historical change shifts further and further away from the direct influence and control of the Valar toward a more independent stance. By the end of the Second Age, conflict over the Rings of Power culminates in the "Last Alliance between Elves and Men," in a decisive battle with Sauron, when the sword of Elendil is broken—a symbol of the beginning of a time of disconnection with the source of guidance and strength. The focus of the Third Age is the dissolution of the now ancient influence of Valinor. The One

Ring lies at the bottom of a river during this time, awaiting the return of Sauron. Interestingly, it lies there for two and a half millennia, which is approximately the same period that Steiner attributes—2,600 years—to each epoch in the evolution of consciousness. Two thousand six hundred years is the period it takes the sun to move through one constellation. This return of the One Ring begins as the final connection with the events of the previous two ages ends:

> But in the wearing of the swift years of Middle-earth the line of Meneldil son of Anarion failed, and the Tree withered, and the blood of the Númenóreans became mingled with that of lesser men. Then the watch upon the walls of Mordor slept, and dark things crept back into Gorgoroth.[81]

With Tom Bombadil we were presented with an image of the atavistic unity of self and world. With Elrond we are presented with an image of separation of self and world. The process by which this separation comes about is history. Evil is the catalyst. Sauron doesn't succeed in winning control of the elves and men but it is through his influence that men finally reach the state of isolation from the spiritual strength and guidance of Númenor and the Blessed Realm. Sauron's strength lies in his ability to disrupt the link between the Valar and the various races of Middle-earth. He is the catalytic force that separates self and world. But he has not yet been able to control the Self. The stage has been set for this possibility at the end of the Third Age.

It is only within this historically imbued understanding of the separation of self and world that Elrond provides a meaningful context for deciding on the fate of the One Ring now in their possession. Elrond makes known to the

Council that the rediscovery of the One Ring is an historical marker that indicates that the time of the Fourth Age is dawning. What happens to the Ring has deep historical consequences as well as personal consequences for the members of the Council and all those who live in Middle-earth.

And so, it is little wonder that it is to Rivendell that the main characters come to reflect on and clarify the most appropriate response to the One Ring. The nature of Rivendell itself reflects the harmony and balance inherent within Elrond's historical consciousness. Elrond has created the right soul mood at Rivendell. The hobbits make the following comments about how they feel being there. I will first share Bilbo's reflections:

> A perfect house, whether you like food or sleep, or story-telling or singing, or just sitting and thinking best, or a pleasant mixture of them all.... Why, sitting and thinking. I do a lot of that nowadays, and this is the best place to do it in.[82]

Pippin also shares:

> It seems impossible, somehow, to feel gloomy or depressed in this place. I feel I could sing, if I knew the right song for the occasion.[83]

Elrond has created an atmosphere in Rivendell that supports reflection, both personal and historical, as well as intense feeling, merrymaking, and productive activity. There is an obvious balance between thought, feeling, and will. Balance is also found in the representation of the peoples of Middle-earth assembled for the Council. Everyone contributes to the deliberations, from the humble to the wise. Eventually a decision will be reached that is a culmination of what everyone thinks about the situation, how they feel about it, and what they think they can do.

Before considering the next form of consciousness brought by Galadriel, we will study the contributions made by Saruman and Gollum (two characters strongly influenced by the One Ring) toward clarifying the nature of modern evil, and, through this, clarifying the focus and direction of the quest. Steiner's understanding of the dual nature of evil—the Luciferic and Ahrimanic polarity—provides us with the right lens with which to understand the role of these two individuals in the story.

Gollum's Ahrimanic Path

Near the beginning of the story, Gandalf gives Frodo an overview of Gollum's character. We learn that he was once a hobbit and came upon the Ring by accident. To possess it he murders his friend, which reveals for us a picture of his soul life. Possession of the Ring leads Gollum to quick ruin: "He became sharp-eyed and keen-eared for all that was hurtful. The ring had given him power according to his stature."[84] He is soon rejected by his community and retreats to the inside of a mountain. Isolated from any positive influences as well as from the rhythmical nature of the seasons and community life, the Ring can act quickly by attacking his thinking, feeling, and willing capacities directly, as Gandalf relates during the Council.

In terms of thinking, Gandalf notes: "The thing was eating up his mind."

In terms of feeling, Gandalf states: "He hated the dark, and he hated light more: he hated everything, and the Ring most of all."

And in terms of willing, Gandalf says: "He could not get rid of it. He had no will left in the matter."[85]

The corruption of Gollum's thinking, feeling, and willing capacities has left his ego in a very fragile, almost nonexistent state. As the Ring corrupts him, he first goes through a hideous soul transformation and then an unusual physical transformation. We learn later that he refers to the small remnant of his original self that still exists by his original name, Smeagol. With his real self almost destroyed by the Ring, Gollum's physical appearance starts to adapt and transform to reflect his unique environment in the darkness of a mountain hole. There is little left of Gollum's inner self to be mirrored in his outer appearance. His physical transformation is the result of this loss of self. The amphibian-like form he assumes reflects his new, dark, moist habitat. There, he also assumes the survival skills of such creatures. The word "Gollum" is the amphibian-like sound he now makes in his throat, indicating his weakening human capacities.

But it is precisely his former hobbit nature (that emphasizes the will) that preserves the last few embers of Gollum's humanity, and therefore his ability to act out his destiny in the quest. As Gandalf reflects:

> Even Gollum was not wholly ruined. He had proved tougher than even one of the Wise would have guessed—as a hobbit might.[86]

This is the reason Gollum inspires such sympathy and pity. Many seem to sense that even though he is ensnared by the Ring, he once had a quite different state of being. Gandalf again comments here: "I think it is a sad story, and it might have happened to others, even some hobbits that I have known."[87]

When he is leading Sam and Frodo into Mordor, Smeagol will resurface and struggle internally with Gollum over his plan to lead Frodo and Sam to their deaths by Shelob the Spider. It's a moral struggle that the reawakened Smeagol, now in the company of healthy individuals and breathing the fresh air of the natural world, won't have the strength to win.

Saruman's Luciferic Path

Our first impression of Saruman is how starkly he contrasts with Gandalf. We would expect that a wizard of higher rank than Gandalf would in some way exemplify goodness. Instead, we find an arrogant, proud, and contemptuous being. Our understanding of him begins with the fact that he lives a stationary and isolated life at Isengard. Saruman is quick to show contempt for Gandalf the Wanderer, one who lives in relationship with the inhabitants of Middle-earth:

> It has seldom been heard of that Gandalf the Grey sought for aid, one so cunning and so wise, wandering about the lands, concerning himself in every business whether it belongs to him or not.[88]

And Saruman adds: "You need not speak to me as to one of the fools that you take for friends."[89]

At Isengard, Saruman has taken on the task of studying the "arts of the enemy." This study had the original purpose of helping to better understand Sauron in order to defeat him. This is partially accomplished when the White Council drives him from Mirkwood. This information gives us some context to begin to see why Saruman has left the path of wisdom. The next clue comes in the image of his wizard's cloak. Its simmering colors no longer portray the wholeness of white but only the separate parts of light—the color spectrum. This disturbs Gandalf, and Saruman responds, as follows:

> "White!" he sneered. "It serves as a beginning. White cloth may be dyed. The white page can be overwritten; and the white light can be broken."[90]

Saruman then explains to Gandalf his rationale for wanting to join the rising power of Sauron, and suggests that with the One Ring they may be able to implement all their long-cherished plans without having to guide the peoples of Middle-earth to uncertain ends. Thus, "Knowledge, Power and Order"[91] could replace guidance and the wisdom that it is based on. Saruman seems to be saying that intellect should be the basis for the order of the Fourth Age. His superior intellect, he now believes, has prepared him to wield the One Ring that he now seeks. Since he has yet to wear it himself, as Gollum has, we can conclude that his growing obsession with it has originated within himself and not from something external to him. He presents his perspective to Gandalf:

> The time of the Elves is over, but our time is at hand: the world of Men, which we must rule. But we must have power, power to order all things as we will, for that good which only the Wise can see.[92]

Saruman's path, to himself at least, becomes as logical and straightforward as a mathematical equation:

> As the Power grows, its proved friends will grow also; and the Wise, such as you and I, may with patience come at last to direct its courses, to control it... There need not be, there would not be, any real change in our designs, only in our means.[93]

As Saruman has isolated himself at Isengard in the tower of Orthanc (a place the Rohirrim call "Cunning Mind"), so we see an image of the isolation of intellect from feeling as fundamental to his chosen path. The "power to order" all things is located for Saruman in the intellect. The order he envisions is one where what is good is something that only the wise can see. What can be penetrated by the power of the intellect only will form the basis of Saruman's knowledge and order, as it does in the contemporary culture in which we live.

Galadriel's Transformational Consciousness

After the Fellowship determine what they will do with the One Ring, they leave Rivendell and face the road to Mordor. Gandalf and Aragorn have considered their options. Given their need for secrecy, two choices exist: either ascend the mountains or descend through the earth. Though the purpose of the quest is clear, its path is not. When they fail in their attempt to scale the heights of the mountain, they have no choice but to descend into the depths. Here we see in the topography of Middle-earth itself a symbolic reflection of the spiritual path they have chosen. There is no longer any direct ascent. Atavistic consciousness once could ascend to the white light of spiritual awareness naturally. In the modern world however, with its emphasis on the development of individual spiritual freedom, the path involves descending into the darkness—the unknown parts of ourselves we must claim and transform if we are to ascend again to spiritual awareness through our own free will. At Rivendell we have seen this modern spiritual path symbolically clarified.

The next segment of *The Lord of the Rings* is the failure to scale Mount Caradhras and the subsequent need to descend into the depths of Moria. On the surface, there seems little reason for this failure other than to dramatically highlight the descent. However, the ascent can also be viewed within the larger theme of initiation. As if to test their decision not to entrust Bombadil with the Ring, the Fellowship chooses the atavistic path represented by a simple direct ascent. Atavistic consciousness was natural to ancient humans. The spiritual world could be accessed directly, so to speak. Having since evolved away from atavism, individuals must transform themselves to attain spiritual knowledge again. This is represented by the descent. The descent into the dark depths of Moria represents our need for self-knowledge, without which we cannot see our own capacities for evil and thus undergo inner transformation. So, the simple ascent is no longer possible for modern humans. The Mines of Moria were once lit and peopled with dwarves, but now lie in a threatening darkness. Its passageways, like human nature itself, are complex and perplexing. Gandalf leads the Fellowship through the dark halls with the symbolic light of thought on the tip of his staff.

Although Gandalf is lost, the Fellowship manages to arrive in Lothlórien, home of Galadriel. Lothlórien contrasts with the earthiness of Rivendell and involves a greater step out of the normal rhythm of life in Middle-earth and into a more transcendent experience of time and reality. Galadriel's magic mirror, which can see into the past, present, and future, is the focal point of the company's stay in Lothlórien, an elven oasis. Whereas Elrond was able to give the context and understanding needed to initiate the Ring

Quest, Galadriel brings the wisdom necessary to sustain it. Once the Company leave Lothlórien it is Galadriel's inspiration that they turn to in moments of crisis. Elrond now fades from the story, as his role in bringing the light of historical consciousness is complete.

Galadriel says that "the Mirror is dangerous as a guide of deeds."[94] This tells us that the mirror experience has more to do with self-knowledge than the immediate practical knowledge needed to continue the journey to Mordor. Galadriel makes it clear that she will not counsel either Sam or Frodo to look or not to look at the mirror, knowing that self-knowledge cannot be forced. The mirror challenges both Sam's and Frodo's personal commitments to the quest. Sam sees the ugly changes happening in the Shire and faces a serious temptation to abandon the quest and return to save his homeland. Frodo beholds scenes from the past and future and is eventually forced to encounter the Eye of Sauron. In its penetrating unblinking stare, the beholder is left naked in their weaknesses and incapacitated. To stand alone and unaided before such a power is hopeless and Frodo's challenge is to experience this hopelessness and yet resolve to continue through trust.

To enable this trust, Galadriel offers the gift of her transformational consciousness by initiating Frodo into a deeper knowledge of the evolutionary plan for Middle-earth. Frodo now learns of something of which:

> It is not permitted to speak.... Elrond could not do so. But it cannot be hidden from the Ring-bearer, and one who has seen the Eye.[95]

Frodo then learns that Galadriel possesses one of the three Elven Rings of Power and uses it to sustain Lothlórien in Middle-earth. But the discovery of the One Ring and the start of the quest have triggered a deep historical change:

> For if you fail, then we are laid bare to the Enemy. Yet if you succeed, then our power is diminished, and Lothlórien will fade and the tides of Time will sweep it away.[96]

Of great significance here is the fact that Galadriel shows the hobbits *images*. Her gift is light, by which Frodo can see at times when "all other lights go out."[97] Both characteristics tell us something about the kind of consciousness Galadriel holds. By revealing the greater dynamics at play behind the unfolding events, she is showing us imaginative cognition at work, and by extension, the need for it. Through her guidance Frodo is now aware of two key facts: first, that standing behind the historical events taking place is a greater transition that will alter the soul life and experience of those left in Middle-earth; and second, that his personal struggle to achieve his part of the quest is linked to the greater changes occurring in the transition from the Third to the Fourth Age.

Galadriel's wisdom lies in the link between self-knowledge and knowledge of the forces that stand behind and direct the historical events of Middle-earth. Just as we have seen a unity of self and world in Tom Bombadil, and in Elrond an understanding of the separation of self and world through history, we now see in Galadriel's perspective a new link between subjective self and objective world. She shows Frodo that these two realities are linked together. If one fails inwardly to resist the Ring, then the outer world will be transformed into evil. If one succeeds, then the world will be transformed into something new. As if to emphasize her role in the story, Galadriel goes through her own moment of initiation when Frodo attempts to give her the One Ring. Unlike Gandalf who asks not to be tempted by the Ring, Galadriel allows the temptation to occur, moves through it and "remains Galadriel."[98] During the temptation she speaks to Frodo of how the Ring would transform her:

> In place of the Dark Lord you will set up a Queen. And I shall not be dark, but beautiful and terrible as the Morning and the Night![99]

Showing her conscious awareness of the process of transformation, Galadriel foreshadows the initiations to come. Her knowledge of the link between self and world allows her to offer the Fellowship the guiding light of transformative consciousness. Where Tom and Elrond fade, we see her presence remain throughout the rest of the story, and indeed arrive at crucial moments.

4c. The Road to Mordor: The Initiatory Experiences of Gandalf, Aragorn, and Frodo

As the Fellowship breaks apart, events lead Gandalf, Aragorn, and Frodo to each encounter a transformative death-like experience. Gandalf will be transformed after his battle with the Balrog of Moria. Aragorn will face the Paths of the Dead. Frodo will face the sting of Shelob the Spider. While the characteristics of these experiences vary, the nature of each is identical. Each character must face and live through an encounter with a potent force that kills off his old self so that a new self can emerge. These experiences form the dramatic highpoints of the whole story. We will examine the specifics of each of these experiences and discover how the soul capacities of thinking, feeling, and willing are portrayed in each. Each experience will be marked by the influence of Galadriel's transformational consciousness, the only remaining help on the road to Mordor.

The Initiation Experience of Gandalf

The account of Gandalf's battle with the Balrog and his eventual transformation into the White Rider creates an important but mysterious image for the reader. On the surface the scene is fast-paced and filled with struggle and action, which has the effect of making the symbolic imagery seem almost subliminal. If we look closely at the structure of the scene and keep in mind Gandalf's role as an image of the soul capacity of thinking, what emerges before us in a kind of template form is the path to imaginative cognition. Gandalf symbolically treads this path in his struggle with the Balrog and therefore experiences on a personal level what he is trying to help accomplish in Middle-earth. His later transformation into the White Rider is an image of his greatly enhanced powers of judgment, intuition, and clear thinking. The battle with the Balrog involves a descent and an ascent inside Mount Silvertine, the geographical center of Middle-earth, which suggests the centrality of this image to the story.

When we carefully examine the sequence, we witness a remarkable series of images that mimic the discovery of the One Ring and its future destruction. Consider the following pattern: Gandalf and the Balrog fall to the bottom of the inner pit of the mountain and land in water, reminiscent of the conditions in which Gollum was discovered. The battle continues through an ascending passageway to the top of the mountain. Gandalf pursues the Balrog much like

Gollum pursued Bilbo out of the dark passageways in the Misty Mountains. At the top they see snow, as the company did on Mount Caradhras. The atmosphere of the mountaintop transforms into "thunder," "lightning," "tongues of fire," and "vapour and steam,"[100] resembling the yet-to-be-encountered Mount Doom. He then "falls into darkness,"[101] just as the One Ring will fall into Mount Doom and be transformed. The mountain breaks apart, as will Mount Doom in Sauron's last gasp of life. Then, alone and naked, as the hobbits will be in the end, Gandalf will be flown away by the eagle Gwaihir, as he will later bare away Frodo and Sam. Gwaihir will take Gandalf to Lothlórien where Galadriel will oversee his final transformation into the White Rider. What characterizes Gandalf the White Rider is the absence of doubt. He no longer needs to gather information and puzzle about the workings of Sauron. He knows exactly what to do because his thinking has transformed from a process of reflection and questioning into a higher perception of how the parts move within the whole. His template experience of the quest and its likely outcome has elevated his powers of thought to that where he can see a picture of the whole and its emerging future. Thus he can say with accuracy to Aragorn, "We meet again, at the turn of the tide. A great storm is coming, but the tide has turned."[102] Had he not now held an enhanced picture of the whole situation, he would have been unable to say that, as he had been absent from the scene.

Gandalf will spend much of the rest of the story moving swiftly to the many large and small players in the drama, orchestrating how they fit into the overall battle against Sauron and knowing full well that the small players, like

Merry and Pippin, can have crucial roles to play. It is this quality of working with the parts and within an image of the whole that characterizes Gandalf the White Rider. He is now able to work from a place resembling Steiner's "imaginative cognition," rather than just from sense perception and factual knowledge. His initiation was a confrontation with an adversary equal in power, as both the Balrog and the wizards of Middle-earth are Maia—higher spiritual beings. His death was the death of his old self, the Grey Pilgrim. We learn later that an important experience occurred just after the Balrog was vanquished. Gandalf's "death" was characterized as a *paralysis of thought*. He was enveloped in cosmic time, where thought is suspended outside the confines of earthly space. This was a transcendent experience from which he was eventually "sent back," suggesting the presence of a higher cosmic intelligence. This experience suggests that thought has a spiritual cosmic nature, as it does in Steiner's anthroposophy. In Gandalf's return as the White Rider, we experience the appearance of the new soul faculty of imaginative cognition. Aragorn, Legolas, and Gimli bow to Gandalf upon his reappearance. As this capacity is not yet a reality in our culture, it appears to us in a numinous light.

The Initiation Experience of Aragorn

After defeating Saruman at Helm's Deep, Aragorn realizes that he will not make the journey to Gondor in time unless he goes by a more direct route. A message arrives from the North: "Bid Aragorn remember the words of the seer, and the Paths of the Dead."[103] Those around him are bewildered that he would even consider taking such a path.

A mountain pass filled with the spirits of disgraced warriors is considered so evil as to be totally abandoned by the living. But Aragorn, knowing he would be able to dispel the curse laid upon them by his heir Isildur, senses that his destiny is taking shape, and he is determined to go.

There are no enemies to face on the Paths of the Dead. On this Path, death comes not from the sword but through fear itself. What saves you is the inner determination not to let the fear overcome you. Aragorn, as an image of the soul capacity of feeling, must face the *paralysis of feeling* that passage through the Paths of the Dead threatens. Near the entrance, the bones of a king lie just off the road and a "notched and broken sword lay by him, as if he had hewn at the rock in his last despair."[104] Aragorn's task is clear: he must not let the kingly qualities he carries in his feelings die. Aragorn has only the inner conviction that his destiny is taking shape as a shield against the onslaught of pure fear.

Identity is crucial to the unfolding of Aragorn's destiny. He knows that only the heir of Isildur can command the dead to fulfill their oath. He bravely navigates the Path of the Dead, then emerges and commands the Host to follow and enter battle for him. It is at this point that Aragorn finally and fully unveils himself as the future King. The Ranger of the North is now gone, as is the Grey Pilgrim. Galadriel's gift of the banner of the White Tree and the Seven Stars is brought to him and he uses it as he takes over the boats of the Corsairs of Umbar, who have been destroyed by the Host of the Dead. Aragorn's identity is now that of King only. He has passed the test of carrying a hidden identity in his feeling life through surviving the paralysis of feeling and now begins its integration into his whole being.

The Initiation Experience of Frodo

Frodo's death-like experience occurs in the clutches of Shelob, the monster spiderguardian of Cirith Ungol, a passage into Mordor. He is stung by Shelob and though Sam thinks he is dead, he in fact is not. Frodo does, however, experience a complete *paralysis of will.* He is unconscious and cannot move. This death-like initiatory experience has been foreshadowed in the attack on Frodo's physical body by the Black Rider's knife. The assault on his body is an assault on his will. Frodo is dependent upon his ability to physically endure the road to Mordor and drop the Ring in Mount Doom. The test of will for Frodo on this road is obvious, as Tolkien notes:

> And sometimes his right hand would creep to his breast, clutching, and then slowly, as the will recovered mastery, it would be withdrawn.[105]

Sam's experience of will is similar:

> But even as hope died in Sam, or seemed to die, it was turned to new strength. Sam's plain hobbit-face grew stern, almost grim, as the will hardened in him, and he felt through all his limbs a thrill, as if he was turning into some creature of stone and steel that neither despair nor weariness nor endless barren miles could subdue.[106]

Frodo eventually stands between Sam's virtue-laden will and Gollum's corrupted will.

The transformation in Frodo is less dramatic and obvious that Aragorn's, but it is still perceptible. After being rescued by Sam, Frodo can cross the threshold into Mordor, his destination. He reflects on the experience:

> As I lay in prison, Sam, I tried to remember the Brandywine, and Woody End, and The Water running through the Mill in Hobbiton. But I can't see them now.[107]

The old hobbit of the Shire who yearned for a hot meal and the comfort of home is gone. His old self was taken in his death-like experience with Shelob. Not surprisingly, Sam finds him "naked" or without his old identity in the Orc tower.

It isn't until Sam and Frodo encounter Gollum at the foot of Mount Doom that we suddenly see the inner transformation happening in Frodo's soul life. In a visionary moment Sam sees Frodo, the physically and mentally exhausted little hobbit, transformed into a vision of inner nobility and power:

> Then suddenly, as before under the eaves of the Emyn Muil, Sam saw these two rivals with other vision. A crouching shape, scarcely more than the shadow of a living thing, a creature now wholly ruined and defeated, yet filled with a hideous lust and rage; and before it stood stern, untouchable now by pity, a figure robed in white, but at its breast it held a wheel of fire.[108]

And:

> We're going east not west. And I'm so tired. And the Ring is so heavy, Sam. And I begin to see it in my mind all the time, like a great wheel of fire.[109]

The fact that Frodo now sees the flaming Ring in his *waking thought* is significant. It represents a change in Frodo's consciousness, achieved through his initiation experience. He now perceives something he could not perceive before. A dim experience of imaginative consciousness has occurred.

Frodo will be unable from now on to perceive the world as he once did. This new reality will set him on a new path to the spiritual world of the Undying Lands.

Frodo's loss of himself in the heart of Mount Doom is, as Flieger observes, the final splintering of the light. Every link to his old self is gone. His inability to let go of the Ring strangely does not interfere with the fulfillment of the quest. It is as much to say that the accumulated effort of his task, faithfully fulfilled up to that point, is all that is needed. Providence will do the rest. Having struggled for so long, it is through grace alone that Frodo wins. In this final moment, the spiritual world makes its presence discernible.

In summary, the initiations of the three main characters are characterized by death-like experiences that result in a transformation of self and identity, in various degrees. They form the dramatic heart of the story, as we witness death produce new life. Each initiation is also a reflection of the soul capacity each character represents, thus reinforcing the centrality of these representations of thought, feeling, and will in the story.

It is interesting to note that in each initiation not only is there a paralysis of one of the soul capacities to contend with, but also a hint of why this paralysis exists. In the case of Frodo's death-like experience, Shelob is characterized as always hungry, much like the hobbits themselves. The hobbits exhibit a tendency to be possessed by a kind of gluttonous preoccupation with food, a tendency brought to the extreme in Shelob. The Paths of the Dead bring Aragorn to a group of spirits suffering the shame of their loss of courage.

They couldn't face the possibility of loss in battle and so broke their oath to their friends. Cursed by Isildur, they await an opportunity to bravely hold to their oath. Aragorn struggles with the feeling of worthiness to assume his high destiny. One senses that a failure on his part will result in an unbearable shame—to have fallen in the same way Isildur did when he could not destroy the Ring. In Gandalf's case, the Balrog is a demon of destructive fire. Gandalf uses the elven Ring of Fire to bring constructive energy to Middle-earth. His task is not to use the destructive force of fire as Saruman does, but to guide with light and with the warmth of deep relationship—the constructive side of fire.

Lastly, there is yet another way to see the relationship between Frodo, Aragorn, and Gandalf in terms of the theme of spiritual initiation. The Western medieval tradition of initiation involved the three distinct stages of bachelor, master, and doctor. This old initiation culture terminology survived in the academic world as the terms used to afford degrees of achievement. The old initiation meaning of "bachelor" was the requirement of celibacy for candidates entering the first stage of initiation. In *The Hobbit* and *The Lord of the Rings*, our two bachelors are, of course, Bilbo and Frodo, neither of whom have the slightest hints of romantic engagement. In Aragorn we see the one other character, aside from Gandalf, who has "mastered" his inner life and steadfastly resists any thought of using the Ring for himself. Gandalf in turn is the real "doctor" of Middle-earth. His task is to heal the wounds of division and diminished consciousness. When Frodo leaves Middle-earth, we sense he is ready to assume the path to the next level, that of "master." His wound that will not heal is the catalyst to greater consciousness. The culture of the Shire is not a place where the next stage of initiation, the "master" level, is nurtured. Frodo no longer belongs there. Sam will begin the slow work of transforming this culture into a place where mastery of the self is valued. Aragorn has already hinted at his next stage. He brings healing through his hands to the sick and wounded, the first steps in the path to the healing doctor. Gandalf, as doctor, has healed Middle-earth; his task is complete and he will no doubt seek other tasks of healing as the Wise deem necessary.

Théoden and Denethor: Human Reflections of the Fate of Gollum and Saruman

After Gandalf returns as the White Rider and unites briefly with Aragorn to defeat Saruman at Helm's Deep, he turns his attention to the King of Rohan and the Steward of Gondor. We discover that both these kings have fallen victim to the same malady as Saruman and Gollum. Now elevated through his initiation experience, Gandalf can identify the problems quickly.

Théoden

We encounter Théoden, King of the Mark, in his darkened Golden Hall. He is bent and worn and unwelcoming to Gandalf, who he sees as the bearer of bad news. By his side is his counselor, Gríma Wormtongue. We quickly learn that Gríma has a strong influence over the King's mind. But it does not take Gandalf the White Rider long to outmaneuver Gríma and expose him as an agent of Saruman.

We learn that Gríma has been able to weaken the King through manipulating his thinking. "Whisperings," "leechcraft," and lies describe Gríma's work. Gríma has worked hard to undermine the King's judgment and isolate him from other influences in his kingdom—from his nephew Éomer (an Aragorn-like character), imprisoned for threatening to kill Gríma. Gríma weakens Théoden by corrupting his thinking, feeling, and willing, and therefore his very identity:

> And ever Wormtongue's whispering was in your ear, poisoning your thought, chilling your heart, weakening your limbs, while others watched and could do nothing, for your will was in his keeping.[110]

Gandalf's reference to the weakened state of thinking, feeling, and willing underscores the central theme they play in the story. It is in the restoration of this balance that Théoden finds new strength and life. He begins again to exercise sound judgment, problem-solving, and decision-making while simultaneously raising the spirits of his people in a call to arms.

Denethor

With Saruman caged and defeated and Théoden riding into battle, Gandalf turns his attention and unifying energy to Gondor and its Lord Denethor. Now Gandalf will unmask and deal with the Saruman Path as it is played out in Gondor. Like Saruman, Denethor has strength and cunning. He spars with Gandalf in a test of wills and puts Pippin through a long and tricky questioning.

As he did with Saruman, Sauron manipulates Denethor's thinking through the Palantir stone. Denethor tries to use the Palantir to his own advantage but as it is partially controlled by Sauron, he only sees what Sauron wants him to see. Denethor slowly becomes overwhelmed by the strength of the forces allied against him. The visions in the

Palantir stone turn his emotional wound at the loss of his son Boromir to despair. When Faramir, his other son, lies wounded and dying, Denethor gives up hope. Like Saruman, he has completely isolated himself.

The Mouth of Sauron: A Combination of Luciferic and Ahrimanic Influences

Gandalf and the Captains of the West decide to confront Sauron at his own gate in the hope of distracting him from seeing Frodo and Sam. At Sauron's black gate they first encounter not a monster, dragon, or Balrog, but simply a man, a human being:

> And his name is remembered in no tale; for he himself had forgotten it, and he said: "I am the Mouth of Sauron."... And because of his cunning he grew ever higher in the Lord's favour.... And he was more cruel than any orc.[111]

Here we have a specific image—a man who has no memory of his original identity. Like Gollum he has lost his identity as a human being. His identity is now synonymous with Sauron's organ of speech, telling us it is Sauron's ego that works through him, not his own. Indeed, it is his sharp intellect, his cunning, which makes him particularly useful to the Dark Lord. Here we encounter a man who stands in direct antithesis to the goals of the Ring Quest. Like Gollum he has no ego-identity left, only a burning lust for power. Like Saruman, "the Mouth of Sauron" displays an active and shrewd intelligence without a trace of emotional resonance or conscience. He is a combination of Luciferic and Ahrimanic tendencies and as such the evil incantation of the One Ring finds full expression in him. He is fully "bound in the darkness" by the power of the One Ring. In his parley with Gandalf, he displays his cunning. He is perceptive and observant. Gandalf feels as if he is "fencing with a deadly foe."[112] He is highly aware and clever. He asks, "Is there anyone in this rout with authority to treat with me... [or] indeed with wit to understand me?"[113] Aragorn locks eyes with him and strives to meet him on the level of feeling. Aragorn wins the contest and the man recoils in fear at Aragorn's emotional strength.

Gandalf is next and displays the "wit to understand" him, first by tricking him into revealing that he does not actually have Frodo captive, and second by stating plainly that this man is a slave and nothing more. The Mouth of Sauron's cunning trap thwarted, he breaks down in a fit of rage, all semblances of his once-human nature gone.

4D. The Road to the Shire: A Conscious Life of Soul

With the quest won and King Elessar's reign begun, the hobbits return to the Shire, where we witness an image of the awakened soul life. The quest has succeeded in destroying the One Ring. At the level of soul experience the ego has successfully initiated and transformed its capacities of thinking, feeling, and willing. The undeveloped and unredeemed aspects of our ego-consciousness that the Ring could control no longer have the power to interfere with the ego's higher development. The Fourth Age begins, the Age of "Men"—human beings without the direct aid of spiritual guides. The elves and orcs have receded. They were symbols of the higher and lower aspects of the ego, external characterizations that have now been integrated into the human being through inner transformation.

In the Shire, Saruman has preyed upon the undeveloped thought, feeling, and will of the hobbits through manipulation and fear. The changes happen slowly at first, unnoticed. They only realize what has been taking place too late. With their rhythmical agricultural life disturbed and no wider awareness of the world to help them, the hobbit culture collapses upon itself. Saruman begins to institute a mechanized culture, beginning with the Mill. Without a conscious relationship to rhythm, the ego cannot nurture its soul life. The beauty of the Shire begins to die.

However, the quest-hobbits have returned to the Shire in a new relationship to their soul life. The quest has strengthened and balanced their thought, feeling, and will. Immediately they see through Saruman's lies with sharp thinking, marshal the courage of their community with strong feeling, and overthrow the intruders in a vigorous act of will—the very work Gandalf said the quest had trained them for.

When Sam restores the trees to the Shire using Galadriel's magic seeds, he is consciously restoring the beauty and rhythmical basis of Shire life. We see yet again the relevance of Galadriel's transformational consciousness to the newly dawning age. The new consciousness in the Shire reflects the fact that the outside world—the macrocosm—is now not a subject of fear and mistrust, as it was at the beginning of the story. Such fear allowed the hobbits to develop a parochial attitude, which shut them off from the positive influences of that wider world.

At the helm of the new relationship between the microcosm (the Shire) and the macrocosm (King Elessar's

Kingdom) are Samwise and Aragorn (King Elessar). The new King no longer needs Gandalf's guidance. His decrees and actions flow out of a new harmony of thought, feeling, and will. What he carried inwardly as regal qualities are now externalized in his actions. The marriages of Sam to Rosy and Aragorn to Arwen signify new life. Sam, destined to be Mayor of the Shire, will be, as Frodo foresees, "whole again." It is his task to be an example to his community of the new, integrated soul life and its possibilities. He is now a spiritual leader as much as a political one.

The end of the story is the bittersweet parting of Frodo and Sam. Sam, the friend of elves, was the untroubled soul with the clarity of purpose to always know the right path when others were in doubt. He was able to carry Frodo when his will was exhausted and to defend Frodo from Gollum, his shadowy lower self. And he could witness to the image of Frodo's transformed soul at the foot of Mount Doom. But that time has passed. Frodo now seeks healing. His experience since the end of the quest has been a troubled one. He continues to carry his wound while the rest of the world heals. Frodo was the only one who momentarily lost himself, his sense of who he is, since he was the one who pit his own will against the powerful influence of the Ring—by being the one to carry it to its destruction. His sacrifice was greater in some way than that of the others. Though he lost, in the sense that the Ring overcame him in the end, he faced the ultimate danger for which Sauron designed the Ring. Frodo cannot enter the renewed rhythms of the new Shire and as such comes to realize that his destiny lies elsewhere. The spiritual realm calls to him, and as he leaves for the Undying Lands, we are left with the hint that Frodo has earned a greater reward.

The last image of the story is one of Sam in his house with his new wife and child, an ordinary scene of daily life. The dramatic war of the Ring is only a memory reflected in the twilight descending on the Shire. The three initiated characters are now gone from his new ordinary life. In Sam's house a light is glowing. "I'm back," he says, and in that simple statement he reveals a confident awareness of place, self, and destiny. As a new husband and a father, he has entered his own new personal rhythms. His life is structured in relationship to those he loves, and out of these rhythms a new drama will no doubt take shape. But it will be new and will contribute to Tolkien's notion that we ascend a spiral as we return to paradise. It won't be as we left it, and we won't be who we were.[114]

4E. A Summary of the Hidden Picture of Spiritual Initiation

The inner form revealed through the lens of Steiner's anthroposophy has a threefold nature. After establishing that the three main characters are representatives of thought, feeling, and will, we experience three kinds of consciousness: atavistic, historical, and transformational. Tom's atavistic consciousness belongs to the past and cannot respond to the threat the Ring poses in the current time. Elrond's historical consciousness allows the Ring to be understood properly in the context of the present. Gollum and Saruman participate in clarifying the threat of the Ring. The Ring enslaves the ego, either by amplifying its weaknesses into a monstrous power or through the inner corruption of the interconnection of thought, feeling, and will. The modern spiritual path is one of remaining balanced between these two forces, a path Steiner identifies with Christ consciousness. Galadriel's transcendent consciousness arms the Fellowship with spiritual insight and gifts so they can embark on the quest. With three forms of consciousness experienced and understood, their orientation to the dangers and mystery of the Ring is completed. Finally, we have the three initiations. As the Fellowship breaks apart, each soul capacity of thought, feeling, and will is strengthened in isolation. This mirrors the way the anthroposophical path brings separate attention and awareness to the transformation of each capacity. Each character must survive the monstrous guardian of their own threshold of initiation and then survive a paralysis of the soul quality they represent. In the end, Gandalf the Grey becomes the White Rider, an image of enhanced thought and knowledge. Aragorn becomes King Elessar, the heart of the new emerging world. But Frodo's change of self is subtle at first. He becomes unable to remember the Shire and thus who he was. Having survived Shelob's lair only with assistance from Sam, he is able to enter his destination of Mordor and complete the task of physically getting the Ring to Mount Doom.

These groups of threes—three soul capacities, three states of consciousness and three initiations—form the inner life of *The Lord of the Rings*. It is this enchanted feeling-perception of hidden pictures that engenders in us feelings that the story is important and valuable.

The weakness of Sauron is that he does not think anyone can resist the power of the Ring, and indeed had not our characters faced the death-like experience of initiation he would have been correct. Sauron underestimates the capacity of unified fellowship, the capacity of humans to freely unite to act out of love for humanity itself, which is a central goal of the cosmopolitan nature of our current phase of the evolution of consciousness, the Consciousness Soul Era.

Collectively the three layers of threefold image form a unified picture of modern spiritual initiation, as described by Rudolf Steiner. Initiation is understood as the achievement of higher consciousness through inner transformation. New consciousness and the transition to it have historically been represented to humanity in the form of mythic images. Mythic image evokes in us a longing for such consciousness. Human beings are designed to achieve the inner growth represented in the story. Thus, the story calls to us and reminds us of who we are and where we are going.

Part 5

Inner Forms, Enchantment, and Meaning

5a. Commonalities Among the Inner Forms

In each of the inner forms we have discussed, some aspect of the meaning and value of *The Lord of the Rings* is present. Each form is pictorial in nature, consisting of a series of images that form one central picture. Patrick Curry's central image is that of an ensouled place where our perception of nature is enlivened by the intersection of human community and spiritual longings. Nature becomes imbued with both human and supernatural spirit. The central Jungian picture suggested by O'Neil and Skogemann is that of a journey through a series of archetypes that mimic the path of personal and collective individuation. The central image revealed through Steiner's anthroposophy is a journey along the modern path of spiritual transformation that enables an engagement with a new consciousness called imaginative cognition.

Each of these inner pictures was revealed through the application of ideas and concepts about human beings to patterns of images that align strongly with the main narrative of *The Lord of the Rings*. These "hidden pictures" coexist in the same story. This supports the idea that a central feature of myth—one missed by the literary lens—is its ability to hold multiple forms of meaning, much in the way that single words once held within themselves a multiplicity of meanings—Barfield's "ancient semantic unity."

Each of these inner forms supports the idea of escape as a response to the world rather than a retreat, as they each hold a picture of the possibility of renewal and positive change. Each contain a forward-looking, hopeful template of a new way of being. Curry's concentric circles counter the separation and objectification of nature into consumable and expendable resources by portraying place as a living entity and source of meaning. The Jungian individuation process counters the one-sided materialism of modern life and its preoccupations with outer realities at the expense of inner realities. Flieger's Barfieldian blueprint to *The Silmarillion* counters the tendency in modern life toward reductionist thinking, atomization and isolation. The anthroposophical view of initiation and transformation counters the notion that human beings are only products of their environment and do not have inner capacities much beyond survival instincts.

Each inner form facilitates the change in perception needed to shift our consciousness into a state of enchantment. The primary vehicle for this shift is image, rather than narrative. The inner forms are pictorial and developed sequentially as the story unfolds; their meanings are felt before they are (if at all) conceptually understood. The discovery of these forms allows us to begin describing our experience of the story in new ways. In discovering the positive, responsive nature of all these hidden pictures, we experience their latent encouraging vision that both ourselves and the world are, as Patrick Curry says, "still mysterious, intelligent, inexhaustible, ensouled."

5B. The Enchantments of Place, Authenticity, Integral Meaning, and Transformation

Enchantment is an experience of altered perception brought on by an emotional engagement with a mythic image or template of mythic images that forms a single resonant picture, something akin to Richard Helm's "resonant image of man." Critical to this description of enchantment is that these images are understood not as the result of a conceptual effort or conscious construction by the author. Instead, the working of inspiration becomes perceptible. It is the mythic image that tells the story. Its effect is to make us more conscious of our own developing and evolving nature and the context of time and place in which our development as a human being is unfolding.

Mythic image, laden with the content of human development, stirs our feelings to the point that we sense something important, even new, is occurring and wish to understand it consciously. We can understand this experience as one of enchantment. Patrick Curry showed us an *enchantment of place*, from which we perceive more deeply the alive qualities of our natural world. The effect is to reorient our values to engage with the aliveness of the world and, as a result, our own inner feeling of being alive.

From the Jungian inner form of individuation, we experience an *enchantment of authenticity*. The template of individuation offers us the experience of what it would be like for our potential to be active rather than passive. We wake up to our potential for self-actualization. The adventure of growth overtakes the fear of change. We pursue more easily the connection to ourselves and others. The inner growth of Gandalf, Aragon and Frodo together offers us a picture of the possible levels of self-actualization. While we identify primarily with Frodo's new authenticity, even he now hungers for a healing, transcendent experience; a new equilibrium to be discovered with Gandalf in the Undying Lands. Authenticity breeds radical change.

From the point of view of Flieger's work, we encounter another enchantment, albeit one that was the result of a conscious application of a blueprint of ideas into a story form. Tolkien's ability to integrate story, language, and consciousness into a living whole result in an *enchantment of integral meaning.* Its microcosmic world, reflected in the dramas that unfold between peoples and individual characters, is the consequence of its macrocosmic realties. We experience a world saturated with coherent meaning. The relationship between cause and effect occurs at a moral level. Good and evil occur at every level of being and are in constant relationship to each other.

From the anthroposophical form we see our individual soul recognize its integral connection to the soul of the world. The change we need to undertake is the change already occurring in the world. The One Ring is bringing about the need for, and hence possibility of, our own inner transformation. The path of dynamic transformation reflects our era of the Consciousness Soul described by Steiner—a time to become aware of our evolving soul nature and our inner capacity to direct that evolution. The anthroposophical inner form engenders an *enchantment of transformation* from which we experience the connection between our individual soul and the soul of the world at the level of consciousness. This transformation is firmly situated in the current time, so we feel the possibilities and opportunities intuitively through our experience of living in the twentieth/twenty-first century. Tolkien, as we have seen, went to great lengths to situate the drama of the One Ring in the context of a particular time. Tolkien took pains to underline the fact that Tom Bombadil's atavism is ineffectual for the quest. The right consciousness for the quest was that of neither Tom Bombadil nor even Elrond, though the quest was brought by Elrond to the present historical moment. Galadriel is the one who assists in the efforts of transformation by supporting each of the main characters in their initiation processes. Her transcendent consciousness is emergent and image-laden, like Steiner's concept of imaginative cognition. We sense from Galadriel not just what is, but what could be.

It is interesting to note that this connection between time and consciousness was the subject of Verlyn Flieger's next book, *A Question of Time: J. R. R. Tolkien's Road to Faërie.* The following is a keen insight worthy of our attention and perhaps one of the clearest statements about meaning and value I have come across. The back cover states:

> Tolkien's concern with time—past and present, real and "Faërie"—captures the wonder and peril of travel into other worlds, other times, other modes of consciousness. Reading his work, we "fall wide asleep" into a dream more real than ordinary waking consciousness and emerge with new perceptions of the waking world.[115]

Enchantments are related strongly to the feeling of reverence. One importance we associate with *The Lord of the Rings* is likely the opportunity it gives us to experience the feeling of reverence. Reverence counters our overly critical intellect, which often needlessly separates self and world. Reverence kindles a sense for the ultimate unity of reality, the integral meaning between our own subjective reality and the objective reality of the world. The continued separation of self and world breeds the pathological materialism referred to by Curry. Our heightened feeling for place, inner authenticity, integral meaning, and transformation, cultivates reverence for life. The hidden pictures within the story foster a living imagination where a "new perception of the waking world" is nurtured.

5c. The Most Comprehensive Inner Form

The quality of meaning that individuals experience from any one of the inner forms is something only individuals can assess for themselves. However, allow me to make a case for why Curry's concentric circles and the Jungian architecture of archetypes subsist within the anthroposophical form (we have already made the connection between Flieger's Barfieldian blueprint and the anthroposophical inner form).

In Patrick Curry's enchantment of place, we are given an image of a new perception of our own natural world, our own Earth. Nature is perceived to be alive, to have its own soul-nature. That new perception is formed when nature (the middle concentric circle) is situated in a continuum between human spirit and supersensible spirit. Enchanted place is the result of the connection between the spirit in the human being and the spirit in the cosmos. Being the middle circle, it holds the qualities of both earth existence and the spiritual world. The earthly world forms its relationship to the spiritual through the intermediary of the middle circle. It is in the place of Middle-earth that the mythological imagery and drama occur in *The Lord of the Rings*. The Shire is sheltered from it and the Undying Lands are not directly involved. As a result, one could also conclude from Curry's inner form that myth is the place where the human being perceives the spiritual world in a kind of disguise, a world of images. This is also a view that is concurrent with anthroposophy. Myth holds images of the evolving consciousness of the human being in relation to cosmic evolution. Myth is the way the microcosm relates to the macrocosm.

The existence of the picture of Jung's individuation process is partially explained through Flieger's idea of splintered light, given that light is an image of waking consciousness and dark an image of the unconscious. Tolkien's decision to hold light as a symbol of wisdom and spirit, and to fragment this light, will inevitably develop into a light vs dark scenario, which in turn is easy to transpose as a conflict between ego-consciousness and the unknown subconscious or unconscious. There seems to be a natural crossover happening in that respect.

But more importantly, individuation can be understood as the preparatory stage of the process of transformation described by Steiner as initiation. Steiner's path of spiritual development is grounded on preparation exercises for moral development. He says that each step on the path of spiritual knowledge requires three steps in the evolution of one's moral character. The initiations of Gandalf, Aragorn and Frodo can thus be seen as a continuum, Frodo's a necessary preparation for Aragorn's, which in turn is a necessary preparation for Gandalf's.

Individuation is the cure for the splitting into light and dark Flieger observes in Frodo's story, as well as for what we experience in our contemporary world, dominated by materialism so that our outer lives are focused on material concerns that dominate our inner lives of soul and spirit. If the Jungian picture of individuation were the foundation of the story, Frodo above all would deserve the fruits of a successful quest. Yet we find him disquieted after the quest. He no longer belongs in the Shire and has not healed. This suggests that the next stage, undertaken by Aragorn and akin to Jung's notion of "self-actualization," is in fact a path that cannot be followed without consciously choosing to do so (as we see in Steiner's anthroposophic path). Unlike individuation, which begins through life's natural challenges, self-actualization proceeds through conscious preparation. It is a conscious modern path of freely chosen inner development. In Aragorn we see the next stage manifest, that of self-transformation. Aragorn has integrated new thinking and new will into his heart forces as King Elessar and has achieved a stage of self-actualization that enables him to serve humanity as a leader. Now he assumes a mythic stature as hinted in his last appearance in the story at the edge of the Shire where he raises the green elfstone so that the sun shines through it, an image of the union of spirit and matter. Gandalf is a stage higher yet. He has spiritualized his ego and fully transformed his consciousness to that of imaginative cognition. The grey doubt of his thinking was overcome. He was then able to act with absolute certainty, directing the overthrow of Sauron with manifest wisdom.

Most of us tread Frodo's path and try to develop the will to forge our own individual, authentic selves in life and to manage something close to an experience of conscious individuation. Many of us are led down this path reluctantly, just as Bilbo was given a nudge outside the door. Trauma, crisis, and hardship are the usual motivating forces, as is unforeseen opportunity. Some of us will reach the stage of fully manifesting our destinies in this lifetime by deeply living into and facing our karmic paths and thus achieve some semblance of self-actualization. To self-actualize is to be a royal figure, a "King or Queen."

Aragorn and Gandalf stand before us as shining lights, a sign of that time when such goals will be reachable for many. They are both numinous, because they represent our future potential, a potential we are able at the present only to feel and imagine, much like Tolkien's description of Faërie as "indescribable yet not imperceptible." Anthroposophy brings concepts to help us perceive this potential and to make it more describable. Central to a description of our future potential is the transformation we undergo when we develop our soul capacities of thought, feeling and will. Gandalf and Galadriel are the only ones in Middle-earth to have obtained this next stage of consciousness, and in the end they leave behind their mythic legends as beacons of hope for the Fourth Age.

Individuation finds a home within the context of an anthroposophical notion of initiation when understood as being a necessary preparation. Individuation can be seen as a transition from the initiation-like experiences life brings our way to our own conscious decision to freely undertake a path of inner transformation.

5D. The One Ring and Evil: Shadow of the Developing Consciousness Soul

The Jungian understanding of the One Ring is a great starting point to discuss this central symbol from an anthroposophical viewpoint. We will recall that the Jungians see the Ring as a shadow of the "Self" archetype. It is the fourth active ring in Middle-earth, when we consider there are three active elven rings. Together these rings form a quaternion, the Jungian numeral of the Self. "It represents the backside of the mandala, the dangerous element that comes forth if the individuation process gets stuck and the Self is not realized and remains unconscious." As Skogemann says, "This is what happened in Middle-earth—as a mirror of our modern world."[116] Skogemann reminds us that the three elven rings fade in their power once the One Ring is destroyed.

> This is not really logical, as they were not made together, but on a psychological level it makes sense. In an individuation process, consciousness separates itself from the unconscious, and so there is a bittersweet parting from the magical world, symbolized by the elves leaving Middle-earth.[117]

This perspective makes a great deal of sense. We can easily see these dynamics at play. The Jungian view sees the rise of Sauron and his power as a consequence of the one-sidedness of both elves and humans, their materialistic concerns, their outer lives seriously out of balance with their inner nature. Sauron can tip this situation to the breaking point by forging the One Ring, which will bind all in darkness. The peoples of Middle-earth will be bound to their shadows.

That the Ring is a symbol of Self, or one might say, ego-consciousness, seems accurate. Its circular form suggests a unity, just as the ego functions in the unity of body, soul, and spirit, and thinking, feeling, and willing. Rings can only be worn by individuals. When we consider the quality of changed consciousness in Frodo, Aragorn, and

Gandalf by the end of the story, it becomes obvious that the power of the One Ring is designed to achieve a corruption of this potential.

The Jungian perspective shows us a duality—ego vs shadow. Yet the story seems to be showing us more than that. The anthroposophical view shows us a threefold image. The Ring forces the individual to hold their ground between *two* polarities of evil, the expansive Luciferic and the contracting Ahrimanic, which have two different effects, a fact not recognized by the Jungian perspective. The Ring can destroy you both ways. The One Ring forces one to struggle with the polarity of evil—a more accurate and detailed representation of how evil works in the story.

The Lord of the Rings has many images of navigating polarities. As discussed, Saruman and Gollum show us the Luciferic and Ahrimanic polarity of the Ring's power. Gandalf the Grey treads the path between Saruman the White (expansion of ego) and Radagast the Brown (contraction of ego). Aragorn treads the path between Denethor (expansion of ego) and Théoden (contraction of ego). His equanimity and inner development neutralize the natural antipathy between Gimli the dwarf and Legolas the elf. Frodo walks the path between Gollum (wanting to steal the Ring) and Sam (wanting to get rid of it and go home).

The One Ring attempts to thwart the emergence of a new form of modern consciousness (the Consciousness Soul, as discussed earlier) that desires to be fully aware of its inner soul-spiritual nature. It is a time when the ego comes to know its full soul nature as a free spiritual being living within the flow of Earth evolution. The ego of the individual strengthens with this knowledge. With this strength comes the greater possibility for egotism—the shadow of the emerging, strengthened, modern, and free individuality. This new individuality is what the One Ring is designed to "bind in the darkness." The One Ring operates as a polarity, attempting through two streams of evil to knock this development off course. Yet, paradoxically, this polarity is the very thing this new individuality requires to develop itself. The destruction of the One Ring after the initiations of the three main characters is an image of the successful development of the Consciousness Soul.

Part 6

The "Secret of the Whole"

6a. Image Over Narrative

"Faërie" is Tolkien's term for the mythopoetic imagination, a form of story whose slow demise he lamented. In 1938, during the writing of *The Lord of the Rings*, he gave an address titled "On Fairy-Stories." In it, he declared:

> Faërie cannot be caught in a net of words; for it is one of its qualities to be indescribable, though not imperceptible. It has many ingredients, but analysis will not necessarily discover the secret of the whole.[118]

Assembling the parts of a mythic story will not reveal why it grips us, especially if those parts are only literary elements. When we venture into mythic story we are disarmed of our words, our concepts. We must allow the percepts to inform us first. It's a phenomenological experience. *Faërie* operates by *its* laws, not ours. In such stories image reigns over narrative. Consider Tolkien's own approach to defining Faërie.

In the same essay he delivered the warning again:

> The realm of fairy-story is wide and deep and high and filled with many things: all manner of beasts and birds are found there; shoreless seas and stars uncounted;

> beauty that is an enchantment, and an ever-present peril; both joy and sorrow as sharp as swords. In that realm a man may, perhaps, count himself fortunate to have wandered, but its very richness and strangeness tie the tongue of a traveller who would report them. And while he is there it is dangerous for him to ask too many questions, lest the gates should be shut and the keys be lost.[119]

Is this statement a description or a definition? Strangely, it seems to be both. Faërie is image, he seems to be saying, not a concept, idea, or technique. Its very nature is pictorial experience, possible only if we maintain the integrity of the whole image. Try to stand outside the image, try to be objective and analyse and look in from without, and the gates are shut. One can't define the "realm of fairy-story" because its definition is image (not imperceptible), not words (indescribable). Rather than define Faërie in concepts, Tolkien simply points to the image.

His description of fairy tales makes me think of the value that Rudolf Steiner placed on fairy tales and myth for children. The inherent morality of fairy tale and myth supports the later emergence of human-centered ethical thinking. The images in the tales undergo a slow digestion and metamorphosis from moral precept to moral concept, but only if the stories can live in the children as whole stories. Explanations kill the images, as Tolkien warned. Enchantment originates in the images, not in our understanding of them. He seems to be saying something akin to this: that the realm of fairy tale is not meant to be understood before its images are digested inwardly, because the very understanding of the images comes from what is digested. Only then can the right concepts arise, informed by our experience and in harmony with it.

Tolkien's sensitivity for the integrity of image over narrative may originate in his agreement with Barfield on the nature of language, perception, and myth. Consider Barfield's full statement of myth:

> Mythology is the ghost of concrete meaning. Connections between discrete phenomena, connections which are now apprehended as metaphor, were once perceived as immediate realities.... As we go back in history, language becomes more picturesque, until its infancy, when it is all poetry; or all spiritual facts are represented by natural symbols.[120]

Enchantment doesn't come easily to our concept-focused consciousness that is used to the constant engagement of abstract thinking and the habit of inattention to perception. Our modern consciousness no longer easily allows the free reign of imagination, nor sees it as having a cognitive value, that is, as a means of understanding the world. I think Barfield would agree with Gandalf when, in his warning to the prideful Saruman, says: "He that breaks a thing to find out what it is has left the path of wisdom."[121]

6b. Tolkien's Personal Images

As we become more aware of the inner forms within *The Lord of the Rings* and how they are essentially made up of mythic images, we may also form a picture of Tolkien's own relationship to image. In 1916, while healing from a serious bout of trench fever after four months in the Somme trenches as a signals officer, J.R.R. Tolkien abandoned poetry as the means to capture his inspirations. His pre-war poems *The Voyage of Eärendel the Evening Star, The Shores of Faëry,* and *Kortirion Among the Trees* had set the stage for the gradual emergence of his own conception of Middle-earth. Instead, he began *The Fall of Gondolin*, the first prose story of his eventual Middle-earth mythology. He named his central demonic figure Melkor, which, in his created language of Quenya, means "He who rises in might."[122] On the subject of Melkor, John Garth, in *Tolkien and the Great War,* observes:

> [Melkor] appeared in 1916 with remarkable timing. With his dreams of world domination, his spies, his vast armies, his industrial slaves, and his "spell of bottomless dread," he anticipated the totalitarianism that lay just around the corner.[123]

Tolkien reports that the story came to him "already fully formed."[124] His anticipation of the twentieth century's totalitarians is a significant moment. He conjured a detailed image of evil that was *future oriented*. This suggests to me that Tolkien was intuiting how consciousness was changing in his time. He would then spend the rest of his life working out the proper form and context in which such an image could be held.

Finally, let us look at the subject of dream. Tolkien reported a recurring dream he called his "Atlantis haunting." He sees a giant wave crest over the landscape of Europe. Jung had a similar dream just before World War I. On this dream, Tolkien wrote:

> This legend or myth or dim memory of some ancient history has always troubled me. In sleep I had the dreadful dream of the ineluctable Wave, either coming out

> of the quiet sea, or coming in towering over the green inlands. It still occurs occasionally, though now exorcized by writing about it. It always ends by surrender, and I awake gasping out of deep water. I used to draw it or write bad poems about it.[125]

We can see in Tolkien's life a strong relationship to image at a very personal level. It seems to me that at significant moments he experienced images laden with an intuitive knowledge. His belief that the whole is a secret that is perceptible shows again the value he places on image as a means of communication.

PART 7

THE VALUE OF *THE LORD OF THE RINGS* AS A MODERN MYTH

The Lord of the Rings is a multifaceted creation brimming with rich, provocative imagery and embedded with a wealth of living ideas and ideals. It nourishes us in ways we will probably never fully understand. We can see inner forms in the story. The nature of these hidden pictures allows us to explore and make sense of our experience of meaning and value. We often encounter vague and confusing commentary on the story's meaning and real value because such content is carried primarily by images not by narrative, by the inner rather than the outer form. These hidden pictures require recognition and understanding.

In trying to understand our common experience of reading *The Lord of the Rings*, commentators began to look to sources other than literary understandings. Jungian commentator Timothy O'Neill eventually presented an understanding independent of literary considerations altogether. This moment allowed for the idea to develop that the story is not fundamentally a literary entity. Hidden within its narrative and literary form lie pictures of meaning. When seen and understood, these pictures allow us to translate our *feeling* of meaning into an *understanding* of meaning.

Remarkably, the hidden pictures show that the creation of *The Lord of the Rings* was not an effort to mimic myth, as is often claimed from a literary point of view. Once the inner forms have been adequately explored, we see these works as an actual living specimen of myth. As Tom Shippey observed, literature in the twentieth century gravitated to the "fantastic" (the imagination) in order to understand the human cost of the acceleration of destructive materialism. Writers worked with imagination as a form of cognizing the nature of this phenomenon. Their imaginations were able to create new forms born from the emergent tendencies of their rapidly changing world. Few of these stories, however, will be read repeatedly. They are beautiful creations, but they lack profound mystery and true mythic character. *The Lord of the Rings* can be read over and over because the inner forms are numinous templates of experience and not because the story's literary qualities are so ingeniously written that they form a superior literary experience. To my mind, if we characterize the inner forms as "numinous templates that nurture a feeling of reverence for life," this provides a new and substantive explanation for the immense appeal the story has in the contemporary world. This will also begin to foster a new relationship with the story. This new relationship to the story has a meditative quality to it, a potential to integrate meaning and experience in ways that strengthen us to meet the future. And that, as Gandalf would say, is an encouraging thought.

Barfield's notion of myth as the "ghost of concrete meaning" suggests that the perception ancient peoples had of their world was based on authentic experience, an experience that then faded and disappeared over time. Their myths therefore were not consciously constructed metaphors applied to erase confusion and ignorance about the natural world or human nature. They were representations of experience. In Steiner's view of the evolution of consciousness, this experience was an atavistic clairvoyance natural to early humans that slowly died out, leaving a legacy of pictures in story form. From an anthroposophical view, myth captures the experience a cultural group has of the connection between their inner life and the inner life of the world they experience.

Building on this idea, we would expect to see in modern myth a similar process, that is, the capturing in pictorial form of the current and emerging state of our self-world relationship. This is what an anthroposophical interpretation of *The Lord of the Rings* reveals. Middle-earth and its War of the Ring mirror our own struggle to subdue the corrupting power of our own egotism that is dangerously nurtured by an increasingly pathological materialism. Our experience of *The Lord of the Rings* is one of a hopeful, future-oriented path.

There comes a time when our relationship to numinous images is integrated into our awareness, and the images' meanings are clarified and their value understood. A new relationship to the story emerges then from our increased understanding of its truly mythic character. This new relationship begins with a feeling of reverence for the mystery of mythic content and its newly revealed intentions. The anthroposophical view of myth shows it has always played the role of holding pictures of a transition into new forms of consciousness. Like Sam at the very end of the story, we stand in a new relationship to ourselves and to the world we inhabit, seeing both with new eyes, encouraged now to make real the possibilities we were shown.

Conclusion

Middle-earth is a world where hidden meaning abounds. Reading Tolkien, we find ourselves distanced from our own seemingly less meaningful reality and, paradoxically, as close to its troubled heart as we have ever been. I have attempted to show a causal link between the anthroposophically based template of initiation—existing as a hidden picture within *The Lord of the Rings*—and Tolkien's conscious working with Barfield's thesis on the evolution of language. In Tolkien's early post-World War I days of mythmaking, he combined Barfieldian-inspired ideas about how language develops with images that came to him naturally. It seems reasonable to conclude that, over time, this activity inspired and gave birth to new images that formed the basis of *The Lord of the Rings*.

The story is popularly known as a literary narrative and not well understood as a container of authentic mythic images. This understanding grows when these images are seen existing in a variety of template forms that foster the inner experience of enchantment. How our feeling of enchantment then translates into a clear understanding of value and meaning depends somewhat, as we have seen, on how we understand the inner nature and hence development of human beings. Different images of the human being can reveal different inner pictures. Knowing the nature of these pictures can then help us explore the reasons why the story resonates for us as individuals.

The goal of this book has been to identify and add to the work that has been done on revealing inner forms within Tolkien's mythic fiction, especially *The Lord of the Rings*. I have tried to make connections between the story's inner forms or "hidden pictures" and the meaning we experience through them. With new clarity as to meaning we are called to reassess and reconsider the nature of the story's true value. I have argued that Rudolf Steiner's worldview of anthroposophy is the lens that reveals the fullest secret meaning of Middle-earth, and it is intimately linked to Tolkien's core motivations for developing his mythology the way he did.

Perhaps the best way to summarize the understanding brought by the anthroposophical perspective is again to reference Owen Barfield. The limited ways of knowing that proceed from a purely materialistic worldview have brought us a "world of outsides, with no insides to them."[126] In response it seems Tolkien has provided us with Middle-earth, a place of immensely detailed "outsides," created with a rare imaginative power and care. His efforts to imbue his story with a semantic unity between perception, word, and story unwittingly created corresponding "insides"—its hidden pictures of enchanted place, authenticity, integral meaning, and transformation. To read *The Lord of the Rings* is to experience a modern myth, a living world of outsides *and* insides that urges and inspires us to reclaim and renew the ensouled reality we know in our hearts is all around us and within us.

Bibliography

Barfield, Owen (1987). "Anthroposophy and the Future." *Towards* 3.1. https://www.owenbarfield.org/read-online/articles/anthroposophy-and-the-future/ (Accessed Aug. 21, 2022).

——— (1984). *Poetic Diction: A Study in Meaning.* 2nd rev. ed. Middletown, CT: Wesleyan University Press.

——— (2012). *History, Guilt and Habit* (2nd ed.). UK: Barfield Press.

——— (1926). "Romanticism and Anthroposophy." *Anthroposophy: A Quarterly Review of Spiritual Science* 1.1. https://www.owenbarfield.org/read-online/articles/romanticism-and-anthroposophy/ (Accessed Aug. 21, 2022).

Carpenter, Humphrey (1987). *J.R.R. Tolkien: A Biography.* London: Allen and Unwin.

Curry, Patrick (2004). *Defending Middle-Earth: Tolkien: Myth and Modernity.* Boston: Houghton Mifflin.

Day, David (2001). *Tolkien's Ring.* London: Pavilion Books.

Flieger, Verlyn (1983). *Splintered Light: Logos and Language in Tolkien's World.* Michigan: William B. Eerdmans.

——— (1997). *A Question of Time: J.R.R. Tolkien's Road to Faërie.* London: Kent State University.

Garth, John (2003). *Tolkien and the Great War: The Threshold of Middle-earth.* London: Harper Collins.

Helms, Randel (1974). *Tolkien's World.* Boston: Houghton Mifflin.

Jung, C.G. (1953). *Two Essays on Analytical Psychology* (Collected Works, vol. 7). Princeton, NJ: Princeton University.

Miller, Seth (2010). "The Spiritual Matrix: An Anthroposophical Reading." *Southern Cross Review*. https://southerncrossreview.org/73/miller-matrix.html (Accessed Aug. 21, 2022).

Noel, Ruth S. (1978). *The Mythology of Middle-Earth*. Boston: Houghton Mifflin.

O'Neill, Timothy (1979). *The Individuated Hobbit: Jung, Tolkien, and the Archetypes of Middle-earth*. Boston: Houghton Mifflin.

Pearce, Joseph (1998). *Tolkien: Man and Myth: A Literary Life*. London: HarperCollins.

Shippey, Tom (2002). *J.R.R. Tolkien: Author of the Century*. Boston: Houghton Mifflin.

Skogemann, Pia (2009). *Where the Shadows Lie: A Jungian Interpretation of Tolkien's* The Lord of the Rings. Illinois: Chiron.

Stein, Murray (n.d.). "On the Importance of Numinous Experience in the Alchemy of Individuation." http://murraystein.com/articles.shtml (Accessed Aug. 21, 2022).

Tolkien, J.R.R. (2000). *The Letters of J.R.R. Tolkien* (3rd ed., eds., H. Carpenter and C. Tolkien). Boston: Houghton Mifflin.

——— (2005). *The Lord of the Rings*. London: HarperCollins.

——— (1977). *The Silmarillion* (ed. C. Tolkien). London: HarperCollins.

——— (1966). *The Tolkien Reader*. New York: Ballantine.

Wehr, Gerhard (2003). *Jung and Steiner: The Birth of a New Psychology*. Great Barrington, MA: SteinerBooks.

Wood, Ralph C. (2003). *The Gospel According to Tolkien: Visions of the Kingdom in Middle-earth*. London: Westminster John Fox Press.

Endnotes

1 Flieger, *Splintered Light*, back cover.

2 Tolkien, "On Fairy-Stories," *The Tolkien Reader*, p. 61.

3 Ibid., p. 64.

4 Ibid.

5 Shippey, *J. R. R. Tolkien: Author of the Century*, p. vii.

6 Ibid., p. ix.

7 Ibid., p. 12.

8 Day, *Tolkien's Ring*, p. 12.

9 Ibid.

10 Noel, *The Mythology of Middle-earth*, pp. 28, 45, 48.

11 Helms, *Tolkien's World*, p. 150.

12 Ibid.

13 Ibid.

14 Ibid.

15 Wood, *The Gospel According to Tolkien*, p. 9.

16 Ibid.

17 Quoted in Pearce, *Tolkien: Man and Myth*, p. 116.

18 Ibid., p. 18.

19 Curry, *Defending Middle-Earth*, p. 105.

20 Flieger, *Splintered Light*, p. 18.

21 Tolkien, "To Robert Murray, S.J." *The Letters of J. R. R. Tolkien*, p. 172.

22 Curry, *Defending Middle-Earth*, p. 152.

23 Ibid., p. 17.

24 Ibid., p. 49.

25 Ibid., p. 50.

26 Ibid., p. 120.

27 Ibid.

28 Ibid., p. 153.

29 O'Neill, *The Individuated Hobbit*, p. 3

30 Jung, C. G. *Two Essays on Analytical Psychology* (Collected Works, vol. 7), p. 171.

31 Tolkien, *The Lord of the Rings*, p. 74.

32 O'Neill, *The Individuated Hobbit*, p. xiii.

33 Ibid., p. 10.

34 Ibid., p. 53.

35 Ibid., p. 70.

36 Ibid., p. 150.

37 Ibid., p. 152.

38 Ibid., p. 70.

39 Ibid., p. 51.

40 Skogemann, *Where the Shadows Lie*, p. 57.

41 Ibid., p. 58.

42 Ibid.

43 Ibid., p. 73.

44 Ibid., p. 157.

45 Ibid., p. viii.

46 O'Neill, *The Individuated Hobbit*, p. 10.

47 Stein, "On the Importance of Numinous Experience in the Alchemy of Individuation."

48 Ibid.

49 Skogemann, *Where the Shadows Lie*, p. 187.

50 O'Neill, p. 160.

51 Barfield, *Poetic Diction*, p. 24.

52 Flieger, *Splintered Light*, p. 35.

53 Ibid., p. 78.

54 Ibid., p. 83.

55 Ibid., pp. 49, 75.

56 Ibid., pp. 75, 58, 135.

57 Ibid., p.137.

58 Ibid., p. 67.

59 Ibid., p. 58

60 Barfield, *Poetic Diction*, p. 90.

61 Barfield, " Anthroposophy and the Future."

62 Ibid.

63 Personal letter from Robert McKay.

64 Miller, "The Spiritual Matrix."

65 Ibid.

66 Tolkien, *The Lord of the Rings*, p. 269.

67 Ibid., p. 170.

68 Ibid., p. 165.

69 Ibid., p. 62.

70 Ibid., p. 191.

71 Ibid., p. 131.

72 Ibid.

73 Ibid.

74 Ibid.

75 Ibid., p. 265.

76 Ibid.

77 Ibid., p. 148.

78 Carpenter, *J. R. R. Tolkien: A Biography*, p. 165.

79 Tolkien, *The Lord of the Rings*, p. 243.

80 Ibid., p. 242.

81 Ibid., p. 244.

82 Ibid., p. 231.

83 Ibid., p. 226.

84 Ibid., p. 53.

85 Ibid., p. 55.

86 Ibid.

87 Ibid., p. 54.

88 Ibid., p. 258.

89 Ibid., p. 260.

90 Ibid., p. 259.

91 Ibid.

92 Ibid.

93 Ibid.

94 Ibid., p. 363.

95 Ibid., p. 365.

96 Ibid.

97 Ibid., p. 376.

98 Ibid., p. 366.

99 Ibid.

100 Ibid., p. 502.

101 Ibid.

102 Ibid., p. 495.

103 Ibid., p. 781.

104 Ibid., p. 787.

105 Ibid., p. 936.

106 Ibid., p. 934.

107 Ibid., p. 918.

108 Ibid., p. 944.

109 Ibid., p. 914.

110 Ibid., p. 521.

111 Ibid., p. 888.

112 Ibid.

113 Ibid.

114 Tolkien, "On Fairy-Stories," in *The Tolkien Reader*, p. 73.

115 Flieger, *A Question of Time*, back cover.

116 Skogemann, *Where the Shadows Lie*, p. 149.

117 Ibid., p. 150.

118 Tolkien, "On Fairy-Stories," in *The Tolkien Reader*, p. 10.

119 Ibid., p. 3.

120 Barfield, *Poetic Diction*, p. 92.

121 Tolkien, *The Lord of the Rings*, p. 259.

122 Tolkien, *The Silmarillion*, Index of Names, p. 340.

123 Garth, *Tolkien and the Great War*, p. 223.

124 Ibid., p. 214.

125 Tolkien, *The Letters of J.R.R. Tolkien*, p. 257.

126 Saul Bellow, dust jacket of Barfield's *History, Guilt and Habit.*

www.ingramcontent.com/pod-product-compliance
Lightning Source LLC
Chambersburg PA
CBHW031338060726
47590CB00007B/2522
9781584208952